the CRAFT of CHRISTIAN teaching

the CRAFT of **CHRISTIAN** teaching

ESSENTIALS for becoming a very good teacher

ISRAEL GALINDO

JUDSON PRESS
PUBLISHERS SINCE 1824
VALLEY FORGE, PA

The Craft of Christian Teaching
Essentials for Becoming a Very Good Teacher
© 1998 by Judson Press

Judson Press, Valley Forge, PA 19482-0851
All rights reserved.

Library of Congress Cataloging-in-Publication Data

Galindo, Israel.
    The craft of Christian teaching : essentials for becoming
a very good teacher / Israel Galindo.
        p.   cm.
    Includes bibliographical references and index.
    ISBN 0-8170-1280-X (pbk. : alk. paper)
    1. Christian education — Teaching methods. 2. Christian education —
Philosophy. 3. Sunday school teachers. I. Title.
    BV1534.G27 1998
    68 – dc21   98-13518

Printed in the U.S.A.

11 10 09 08 07

5

To all my teachers

Special thanks to
Timothy Brock, Sam Compton, Art Hazlett,
Jean Matthews, Brenda Overby,
Barbara, Doug, and Thomas
and
the Community of Faith that is
Vienna Baptist Church
who practice the craft authentically

Contents

Part 4
THE CRAFT

Part 5
METHODS

APPENDIXES

THE CRAFT
of CHRISTIAN
TEACHING

Introduction

There are certain times in our lives when, for whatever mysterious reason, we stumble into a new state of awareness — about self and the way the world works; perhaps even about God, ultimate reality, and what it all means. Sometimes it's the result of a cosmic convergence of the right moment, the right setting, the right need, and the right teacher. As the saying might be phrased, "When the student is ready, the teacher will come." With eerie clarity, I can recall that in all my personal episodes of new awareness, a teacher has been there. They weren't all teachers by office or title, of course, but many of them were.

As any Christian educator in the church setting soon discovers, one of the most critical components in the health of a church is the quality of teaching that is available to its members. Yet one of the perennial struggles for churches is the recruitment and training of teachers for educating children, youth, and adult members in matters of faith. With the increasing difficulty of training teachers in the craft of Christian teaching, the need to staff our church educational programs often degenerates into a matter of finding a warm body for a classroom or securing at best a sitter for children coming to receive Christian instruction. Sadly, many churches still seem to see the role of Christian teaching as secondary to the life of the church. Participation in learning is seen as an optional activity of little or no consequence to the spiritual or personal development of the members.

This flies in the face of the Search Institute's 1990 findings from their national study of Protestant congregations. In their summary report titled *Effective Christian Education*, the researchers concluded:

Christian education, then, takes on new importance. Done well, it has the potential beyond any other congregational influence to deepen faith and commitment. Knowledge of its importance makes the need for educational revitalization all the more urgent. There is much work to be done. The fact that involvement in Christian education ends for most Protestants at the 9th grade is only one problem. Equally serious is the fact that those adolescents and adults who choose to participate are not often exposed to particularly effective programming.[1]

I am convinced that one of the most critical ways of ensuring an effective Christian education in the local church is by training effective teachers. Trained clergy and professional church educators can do only so much. Indeed, some of my most significant moments of new awareness about self and God were a direct result of the work of a dedicated and skilled lay teacher. Most church teaching is done by volunteer teachers, many of whom often have little understanding of the nature of Christian education and sometimes even less training in the craft of Christian instruction.

This book will help Christian teachers by providing a basic orientation to an authentic approach to the craft of Christian teaching. Within that framework the book leads the reader from considering foundational issues of Christian teaching to practical matters on the craft of Christian instruction. At the heart of this book is the question of what are authentic skills and approaches to Christian instruction in the local church and related settings. Throughout the book, these fundamental questions are addressed:

- Is Christian teaching essentially different from other forms of teaching?

- Are some approaches to Christian teaching more appropriate than others?

- Is there a different way of learning that more effectively impacts matters of faith?

- What skills in the teaching craft does the Christian teacher need to possess for effective instruction in the church?

- Which methods of teaching are most consistent with an authentic approach to Christian instruction?

To discover the answers to these questions for yourself, you are encouraged to consider the Points for Further Thought at the end of each chapter. This critical exercise will help you apply the ideas found in the book to your own teaching ministries. As a teacher, I can think of no more gratifying feeling than knowing that when a student was ready, I was called to enter into his or her life to help bring about life-changing learning. That calls for commitment to the task of being the best you can be at the craft of Christian teaching.

Note

1. Peter L. Benson and Carolyn H. Eklin, *Effective Christian Education: A National Study of Protestant Congregations: A Summary Report on Faith, Loyalty, and Congregational Life* (Minneapolis: Search Institute, 1990), 2.

Part 1

Foundations

Chapter 1

What They Don't Tell Us about Christian Teaching (Which We Didn't Want to Hear Anyway)

When I was called to my first church staff position as "resident educator," I had already worked in several educational endeavors, but not in the role of a "Christian educator." So, as any smart person would do, I went out and did some homework. I found myself reviewing books, programs, and journals for hints and clues about "frameworks" and "approaches" for doing Christian teaching. It was very helpful. My informal but diligent research confirmed what I suspected from the start: *you won't find the answer in the books.*

Loren Mead, founder and former executive director of the Alban Institute, recently shared the following insights at the launch of the Center for Creative Leadership Development in Virginia. He named twelve "theorems" for working with churches. I find them to be apropos to Christian education. "These are truths you did not want to know," he told his audience. "We don't admit this stuff."[1] Here are his "theorems":

1. *Nothing works.* "Don't worry if it ain't broke; pretty soon it will break."

2. *Almost anything can work a little bit better.* "Commit to making something work...tinker with programs."

3. *There are no easy answers.* "There is no quick fix."

4. *There are no quick answers.* "We want something like a shot from a doctor. Take it and you're well."

9

5. *There may not be an answer.* "Many problems [in the local church] have no one answer."

6. *There is no such thing as strategy, only tactics.* "Life happens too fast to get long-term clarity and have a long-term plan. . . . Learn to live experimentally."

7. *There are no big deals anymore.*

8. *Money won't solve your problem.* "The problem isn't the money; it's having the initiative to do something."

9. *A new _____ won't solve your problem.* "You fill in the blank — pastor, deacon, [staff member]. Talk as if somebody new from outside will solve your problem and you dodge the issue.

10. *You can't get there from here.* "In times of change, by the time you figure out where you want to go and organize yourself to get there, 'there' has moved."

11. *You won't get anyplace if you don't start from here.* "Ministry is here and now, not in the future."

12. *Ministry is the journey, not the destination.* "Ministry is now, and the task of helping people enter into leadership in [Christ] is the radical reality that this is it."

Depending on how you hear them, Mead's theorems can either be discouraging or motivating. I find them exciting because they strip away the illusions of trying to build a "perfect Christian education ministry" (or youth ministry, or children's program, etc.). That perspective allows us to roll up our sleeves and do the work with more integrity. I've shared similar thoughts on Christian education to effectively talk myself out of a job with interviewing churches seeking a minister of education to come "fix" their program!

So what does this say to us as we look to build an effective Christian education program? Well, for starters (with apologies to Dr. Mead), here are *Dr. Galindo's ten "theorems" of Christian education:*

1. *Stick to the basics.* If you don't know what the basics are, you'd better find out, *fast!*

2. *Decide who you are before deciding what you'll do.* That's good advice for living as well as for Christian education. Christian teaching flows from who you are in relation to God and others, not from how well you can perform.

3. *Process is more important than content.* 'Nuff said for now; more on this later.

4. *No curriculum will solve your program problems.* "If we could only get the right curriculum for our church, we would have an excellent Christian education program, and all our problems would be solved." This is one of those amazingly tenacious myths that seems never to go away.

Curriculum writers are like horoscope writers. Ever wonder how your horoscope is so accurate (that is, if you care to admit you read it)? Try reading someone else's horoscope, on any day. They are written so generically that more than likely you'll still feel they are talking about you.

Curriculum publishers, because they have to sell to such a broad audience, write in ways that will appeal to the "average person in the pew." Whatever that means! I always thought we were all created "unique and special." So how can you write for the average person? I never think of my church's teachers, children and youth, or adults as "average." I think we're pretty special and above average in our church. Don't you believe that about *your* church?

What a good curriculum will do for you is provide structure, offer ideas, give some biblical interpretation and cultural background information, and suggest a starting place for your teaching. But here's what it won't do for you: inspire you or your students, make you a better Christian, meet the particular needs of your learners, or solve your classroom problems. Curricula are written to be sold to the widest possible audience. You're special. Your class is unique. They don't write curriculum for you.

5. *You can't teach anybody anything.* But people learn. Good teachers facilitate learning; great teachers *inspire* learning.

6. *People don't remember lessons.* They do remember relationships. Even after people die, relationships go on forever — that's why people grieve. Are you concentrating on lessons or relationships?

7. *There are just so many ways people learn.* People have only five senses through which they learn (well, actually nine or twelve depending on who you talk to, but that's beside the point). "Creativity" and "innovation" go only so far before they become ineffective.

8. *Learning never ends.* It's a lifelong adventure. When you stop learning, you start dying; and you'll never learn it all!

9. *There is no perfect program.* So quit trying to find it! There are good and better, valid and sound, and great and good enough. And any one of them is only good for its time because people grow and times change.

10. *Learning is change.* Teaching is not entertainment; learning is not always fun. Change is difficult, sometimes painful, often resisted. The kind of change (learning) we seek in Christian teaching at its highest level is *metanoia*, "conversion." In the final analysis, that's the work of the Spirit, and that's *real* change!

Points for Further Thought

- One of the axioms presented is "You can't teach anybody anything." Do you agree? Why or why not?

- Why do you think it would be important to know who you are before knowing what you'll teach?

- If a new teacher asked you what three basics in Christian teaching he or she should always remember, what would you say they were?

- If you were asked to write this chapter by providing your own "Ten Axioms for Christian Teaching" what would they be? Write them down.

Note

1. "12 Theorems for the Church," *Religious Herald* 167, no. 13 (April 14, 1994): 5.

Chapter 2

What Makes
Christian Education Christian?

At a conference gathering of educators, talk around the lunch table turned to matters of a heady philosophical nature. As often happens when a group of professional practitioners gets together, the most heated debates were not over techniques or technologies, but over the more essential matters. While munching on a sandwich, I watched as two schools of thought emerged. What began as a pleasant social conversation soon turned into a debate. A group of professionals sitting at one lunch table turned into two opinionated ideological camps, and by the end of the lunch break, people were sitting at separate tables!

Watching that interesting scenario, I was reminded how I've never understood why some people think philosophy is boring; it seems that the more ethereal the subject at hand, the more heated the emotions. People have gone to war over theology, and ideologies have spawned revolutions.

The question of what makes Christian education "Christian" is an ongoing debate. This is a foundational question, and as such it may not have any one *right* answer; so the debate will continue long after you finish reading this chapter. But, sooner or later, every Christian educator and teacher realizes that this question needs an answer. If you are called to teach you don't have the luxury of not having to think about it. And settling for a Forrest Gump approach to answering the question ("Christian education is as Christian education does") won't carry you in the long run.

At the heart of the argument regarding the nature of authentic Christian teaching is the question of uniqueness. Is there really something essentially different about teaching that is Christian? Ian A. Muirhead wondered: Can we regard Christian education "as a hybrid, composed of education — itself a purely secular technique — and of Christianity, drawn from another source, rather artificially put together to serve certain demands made sociologically on the church? Do we look upon it as the application of a certain kind of know-how to the practical needs of the Christian community? Or can we say something different about it?"[1]

Any educational endeavor is at heart a socialization process, regardless of where or when it takes place. Whether you teach in a preschool, public elementary school, high school youth group, adult Sunday school class, private Christian school, or a state university, in the end, the goal of the intentional educator is to help persons *become.* That is the awesome power and terrifying potential of education — not to make "smarter" persons, but to help shape and make "different" persons, hopefully, better persons.

Christian teaching is similar to other forms of education in that it also intentionally helps persons *become.* It is essentially different, and becomes Christian, when it redefines the basic educational categories of context, content, approach, outcome, and methods and in distinctive Christian terms. Using these classic educational categories, an authentic Christian education approach for teaching might be described as follows.

Context

The context in which Christian teaching happens is not so much a "school" as it is a community of faith. Jesus did not establish a seminary to train his disciples to carry on the work of the gospel. He sent the Spirit to birth what the apostle Paul called a "mystery" — something essentially new and different from anything that ever existed before. A community is where we learn who we are with the help of others; it is where our vocational identity is not so much found as it is negotiated with the help of others.[2] Most importantly, community is where we are mentored and taught the skills of how to make meaning in life.

Content

Traditionally, the answer to the question "What is the content of Christian education?" is: the Bible. After all, that's what we all grew up studying in Sunday school if we were faithful churchgoers. But we contend that a more legitimate answer is: *the person of Jesus Christ.* As we examine the content of the Bible, and especially the New Testament, we discover that *its* content is the person of Jesus Christ. The Gospels and Epistles are literary samples of the continual struggle to know, understand, and be in relationship with Jesus of Nazareth. So the legitimate *primary* content of Christian teaching is not a text, or a creed, but a person!

Approach

Educationally speaking, our approach refers to "the way we go about" doing the work of teaching. Given that the context of Christian education is a faith community, and given that the content is a person; then the approach needs to be relational as opposed to purely didactic. You can teach a lesson, a book, a concept, an idea, or a subject. You can't teach a person; you can only be in relationship with a person.

The most damaging uncritical assumption that exists in Christian teaching today is that teaching *about* God is tantamount to providing an experience of God for learners. To sit under what commonly passes for Christian teaching is to witness the unquestioned notion that *teaching about what the*

Bible says about Jesus of Nazareth is tantamount to introducing Jesus to learners on a personal level. Tragically, that is a perfect description of adolescent cognitive egocentricity: the assumption that to know about something is to comprehend it. When it comes to matters of faith, that is a very dangerous assumption.

Outcome

In a traditional schooling model or approach, the outcome is mastery of the text or content. But if the content of Christian education is a *person,* then mastering someone makes no sense. Since the approach in Christian education is to be in relationship with the person of Jesus Christ, then the outcome in teaching is to be changed by that relationship, to continue to deepen that relationship, to *become* as a result of that relationship.

Methodology

Traditional models of education use schooling and laboratory methodologies to realize their instructional outcomes. But a Christian education that has a person for its content and being-in-relationship as its driving dynamic approach cannot function within the boundaries of a schooling model. As Morton Kelsey said, a Christian education that is genuine must use methodologies that are Christian.[3] The more legitimate methodologies for Christian teaching, then, are those relational approaches in which Christian education happens within the context of the faith community.

The chart on the following page summarizes the comparison and contrast between a traditional educational approach and the approach that answers the question: What makes Christian education "Christian"?

	Traditional Schooling	Christian Education
CONTEXT	Schooling or classroom	Community of faith
CONTENT	Text or creed	Person of Jesus Christ
APPROACH	Didactic or instructional	Relational
OUTCOME	Mastery of content	Becoming while in relationship
METHODS	Schooling or laboratory	Dialogical

Points for Further Thought

- Which approach does the environment in which you teach favor?

- If you were to change your teaching approach toward a more relational one as described above, what would you change about your teaching?

- How do you think your learners would respond to your change in teaching approaches?

- Can you compare and contrast three teaching methods appropriate for each of the approaches: schooling and Christian education?

- How valid, do you feel, is an argument for a unique approach to Christian teaching?

Notes

1. Ian A. Muirhead, *Education in the New Testament* (New York: Association Press, 1965), 15.

2. James Fowler, *Becoming Adult, Becoming Christian* (San Francisco: Harper & Row, 1984).

3. Morton Kelsey, *Can Christians Be Educated? A Proposal for Effective Communication of Our Christian Religion*, comp. and ed. Harold William Burgess (Birmingham: Religious Education Press, 1977), 9.

Chapter 3

Instructional Implications from Learning Theories (or How to Use What the Experts Know)

I can trace my intrigue with Christian education to one single moment. That moment was when I stumbled upon a statement by Morton Kelsey that went something like this: For Christian education to be authentic, its approaches need to be Christian also.[1] That did it! From then on, the search began to find legitimate methodologies for an authentic Christian education.

Learning and teaching are not equivalent: either can occur independently of the other, and frequently does. Your approach to instruction will reflect in great measure your concept of how the human mind works and how we learn (your epistemology). As Christian teachers we need to use those instructional methods that will most effectively help our learners incorporate the truths of God's self-revelation into their minds and hearts.

All methods are not equivalently effective for all teachers: part of the artistry of teaching lies in discovering those strategies most appropriate for *you* as a teacher, *your* student, and *your* lesson. Instructional intent, physical environment, resources — these and many other factors enter into your decision to use a particular teaching approach. Educational research in learning theories can be of great help to us in our work of Christian teaching. Below are discussions of two instructional implications based on educational research: task analysis and meaningful learning.

Task Analysis

Early attempts to discover the mechanisms of learning were frequently frustrated by a fixation on finding the *one* way to teach. Whether the task was learning to tie one's shoe, solve word problems in arithmetic, or write a college term paper, educators assumed that "how" was largely independent of "what."

Then Robert Gagné, in *Conditions of Learning,* argued that different instructional methods should be used according to the demands of varied particular learning challenges.[2] ("A blinding flash of the obvious," you say. Maybe, but he said it *first.*) He categorized the most common reasons why we teach, reasoning that clarifying desired outcomes should help in the choice of effective methods. Gagné listed five distinct "varieties of learned capabilities." These represent the purposes for which teachers provide instruction:

1. to impart basic intellectual skills ("procedural knowledge")

2. to extend verbal information ("declarative knowledge")

3. to facilitate development of cognitive strategies

4. to develop attitudes

5. to enhance physical motor skills[3]

Simply put, by clarifying the objectives for your teaching, you the teacher, can better select teaching strategies. In other words, if you know *what* (content) you want the learner to learn, you can select the most effective *how* (method).

The first three varieties of learning in Gagné's list constitute a hierarchy called cognitive learning. At the lowest level, students acquire information by processes similar to those used in classical operant conditioning (remember Pavlov's dog). Following directions and learning the names of letters and numerals represent what Gagné calls "signal learning" in which specific stimuli-response associations form between the visual or aural cue and a specific behavior. Combining or "chaining" several simple actions represents the next level; the result may be either a verbal chain, linking words, or a procedural chain of sequential actions to perform. When you learned to recite the pledge of allegiance or learned to follow a set of instructions to start a car, you learned by chaining.

For these simpler levels of learning, teachers will find elements of behaviorism, such as drill and reinforcement techniques, appropriate. But much classroom learning, and much of what we really want to see happen in Christian teaching, involves more complex demands. Students must be able to classify groups of items or facts, form concepts, deduce rules to link concepts, and apply these rules to solve problems or evaluate issues. Use of *demonstration* and similar elements of *social learning theory*[4] prove more effective at this level, and students may begin to initiate their own strategies for achievement.

Meaningful Learning

Learning theorists often look down on instruction aimed at direct impartation of knowledge. This aversion to "telling as teaching" has empirical grounding; studies indicate material learned by rote is quickly forgotten. David Ausubel's theory of verbal learning suggests, however, that retention improves when material becomes meaningful to the learner. His strategy stresses the use of "advance organizers" to enhance meaning. Advance organizers consist of information provided in advance of a lesson to help students store and retrieve learned material. In your teaching, this preliminary information might include definitions for concepts and terms in the lesson; analogies, anecdotes, or visual models; or generalizations that provide a framework for the detail that follows.

Advance organizers work because they facilitate both assimilation and accommodation of lesson content, both of which are higher order cognitive functions. According to Ausubel, the single most important factor influencing learning is what the learner already knows. The effective teacher will try to ascertain this and teach the learners accordingly.[5]

This is why learning "facts" has its place in Christian education. Knowing place names, names of countries, names of Bible books, memorizing verses (and, yes, even dates) are foundational; they are what learners need to build upon. But they become significant only when they have meaning to the learner or help the learner in making meaning. In your teaching, advance organizers can help you teach foundational information (facts) more effectively and in a way that the learner can value.

Whether you realize it or not, your choice of teaching methods flows from your convictions about the nature of human mentality. Understanding what behavioral research says represents one vital component of good pedagogy. Effective teachers incorporate significant learning principles in the artistry of their ministry. But in deciding what to teach as well as how to teach, the Christian teacher relies on a biblical understanding of human personality. Empirically derived theories become appropriate only as the teacher applies their constructs within an integrated philosophy of teaching. (You might want to consider what your own integrated philosophy of teaching is.)

The demands of Christian teaching never prove to be easy. Our mandates of evangelism and discipleship demand the use of maximally effective methods. Maturity in this vocation of teaching (professional or volunteer) is evidenced by the increased ability on the part of the teacher to facilitate a learning process that brings out the creative uniqueness with which God invested each learner. This is essentially the art of teaching.

Points for Further Thought:

- Which teaching methods do you tend to use the most?

- Read Gagné's five purposes for instruction. Which relate most to Christian teaching? Do any not relate to your work with your learners?

- In two sentences each of seven words or less, write your personal philosophy of Christian teaching.

Notes

1. Morton Kelsey, *Can Christians Be Educated? A Proposal for Effective Communication of Our Christian Religion,* comp. and ed. Harold William Burgess (Birmingham: Religious Education Press, 1977), 9.

2. Robert Gagné, *Conditions of Learning* (New York: Holt, Rinehart and Winston, 1965).

3. Ibid.

4. Julian B. Rotter, *The Development and Application of Social Learning Theory,* Selected Papers, Praeger Special Studies (Westport, Conn.: Praeger Publications, 1982).

5. David Ausubel, "Use of Advance Organizers in the Learning and Retention of Meaningful Verbal Material," *Journal of Educational Psychology* 51 (1966): 267–72.

Chapter 4

The Formula: Learning = Change

When I taught in a college degree completion program, I started every course or seminar by trying to help my students understand "what learning is." This was important for several reasons. First, most of the students in the program were adults who were returning to college in midcareer (and midlife). For many of them, schooling and college were associated with a personal failure. Many had become convinced that they were not "good learners."

Second, our educational approach had no tests or exams. Students were expected to be responsible for their own learning and had the responsibility of communicating what they learned at the end of the course through dialogue, essays, debates, projects, and other means. This is in contrast to more traditional schooling approaches that require the student to give evidence of having mastered what the teacher was trying to teach by giving the "right answers" to scripted questions. The majority of students genuinely struggled with understanding "what learning is." After all, if they didn't know what learning is, how would they know if they had learned anything?

To help my students grasp the concept of learning, I introduced them to my formula on learning. It's a simple formula designed as a starting point upon which the students would build their concept of learning. It looks like this:

$$L = \frac{C}{(k, a, b)}$$

In this notation, L = learning; C = change; k = knowledge; a = attitude; and b = behavior. Simply, the formula expresses the idea that in essence learning is change. Within the learner, change takes place in three domains: a person's attitude (values), knowledge, or behavior. Of these, knowledge is the easiest to change, and attitude is the most difficult. Underlying this concept is the acknowledgment that where there is growth, there is change.

Merely "receiving new information" is not a sufficient definition for learning. After all, if we see a teacher give a student a textbook containing new information, we would not say that the student actually learned anything just by accepting (receiving) the book full of information. He or she would have to open the book, read the information it contained, manipulate the information, understand it at some level, process it, and then apply it somehow (either theoretically or practically).

Yet, it is surprising how often we as teachers are lulled into believing our learners have learned something just because they have received some new information or fact. The truth is that learning is change. How do you know someone has actually learned something? Because there has been observable change in the person.

Change can occur in a number of domains. Observable change can occur in a person's knowledge, or attitude, or behavior. The effective teacher does not merely hope that changes will occur in any one of these domains; the effective teacher intentionally directs learning experiences to bring about change in the lives of his or her learners. Below are some guidelines to help you teach for change:

- Determine the change in the lives of your learners that your teaching will call for (remember the purpose of advance organizers?)

- Write a learning objective that focuses on that change in the domains of knowledge, attitude, or behavior. For example, "By the end of this lesson, the learner will be able to recite the Ten Commandments."

- Teach one thing (a truth, a skill, a concept, etc.) and one thing only per lesson.

- Teach to effect change in one domain primarily (knowledge or attitude or behavior).

- Use learning methods that will help the students reach that objective.

- Determine how the student will demonstrate that learning has taken place. (What change and in which domain will it be evident?)

Learning equals change! The effective teacher plans and teaches not just to share information, but to change lives.

Points for Further Thought

- If it is true that learning equals change in knowledge, attitude, or behavior, can you say that you've learned today?

- Think about your next teaching opportunity. Can you identify any change in attitude (values) you will call for in your learners? Can you identify any change in behavior you will call for in your learners? Can you identify any change in knowledge you will call for in your learners?

- Think about what you know about Jesus as a teacher. Do you think he subscribed to the idea that learning = change? Why or why not?

Part 2

Frameworks

Chapter 5

Two Frameworks
for Christian Teaching

Whenever our family drives by a building construction site, my kids crane their necks out the window to spot the "Christmas tree." The next time you go by a construction site, keep an eye out for the evergreen tree. You'll find it on top of the building's framework. When a building's framework is completed, the construction crew will put an evergreen tree on the apex of the building. It's an old custom meant to bring good luck.

Frameworks are important; they provide the basic structure that gives form to the building. Foundations are what we build on, but only when the framework is in place do we get a hint of how a building will look when it's completed. Walking through the skeletal structure, we can readily identify where the rooms will go. With only an outline of wood and metal we can imagine how a room will look and feel.

A characteristic weakness of Christian teaching in local churches is a lack of intentional awareness of what framework is best for a particular church or faith community. In fact, how many church educators do you imagine can define the educational approach used in their church? Frameworks (which include strategies, goals, and choice of content used in Christian education) are the outworking of the nature and identity of the church. A church's particular framework for Christian teaching, the way it goes about educating its members, must flow out of its self-understanding.

Our understanding of the nature of Christian teaching determines how we work it out. Basic assumptions about the nature of the *learner* lead to how we define the role of the *teacher*.

What we determine to be the *goal* of the Christian education experience determines the *scope* and content of our curriculum. And in turn, our understanding of the nature of our faith community, our church, determines what our Christian education goals will be.

As you examine the following traditional frameworks, reflect on which you feel best describes the Christian teaching program of your church or organization. While there may be some overlap and generalities in the following descriptions, they will serve to provide a way for you to compare and contrast two different frameworks for Christian education.[1]

Religious Instruction

An ancient and traditional framework for Christian education is called *religious instruction*. This framework has been the backbone of Christian discipleship in the church since the first century. The *goal* of this approach is to transmit Christian religion, understanding, and practice to believers. The *learner* is viewed as an individual with developmental and personal needs and interests that can be met by the content of religion. The *teacher* in this approach serves as the one who structures the learning environment to facilitate the learning of religion. The usual *setting* for learning is a formal, structured, didactic environment, like a classroom.

In this framework the *content* of religious instruction is the Christian religion itself. Theology, doctrine, core beliefs, practices, Scripture, history, faith stories, and dogma form the content of what is relayed through instruction. The curriculum allows the teacher to structure the learning environment to help the learner to acquire and retain Christian religion.

Strengths and Weaknesses: Certainly a strength of this approach is the serious attention given to the perpetuation of the church's core teachings. There is a stress on the application of educational research to the life of the church, with an emphasis on teaching skills. A major weakness in this framework is the expectation of a higher level of teaching competence than may be present in most churches. Also, there is the bias toward more formal educational settings and the learning of content as an end in itself. Critics of this approach decry it as a "banking" approach to education in which the learner becomes an uncritical depository of knowledge.

Faith Community

A contrasting framework for Christian education is the *faith community* approach. In this expression of Christian education the *goal* is to form the congregation into a community where persons can encounter the faith and learn its lifestyle. The view of the *learner* is that of a person struggling to identify with the Christian community and incorporates the congregation as a group of people seeking to be faithful to their identity and calling. In this framework, the *teacher* plays the role of a "priest" — one who interprets and mediates in the community. The *content* with which the teacher works is the Christian community's faith and lifestyle.

The *setting* for learning in this framework is the life of the community of faith itself — its practices, cycles, customs, culture. Through the curriculum, the teacher-priest enables the congregation to seek to be faithful and exposes the "catechumens" to learning points in the life of the community of faith.

Strengths and Weaknesses: A significant strength of this approach is its validation of the community nature of the church and its overarching, all-encompassing educational settings. One major obstacle in this approach is the difficulty of intentionally using enculturation structures for Christian education and positive growth and change. Another hazard is the assumption that a community of faith is always faithful to its nature and calling, and that it enjoys a redemptive level of institutional health.

Both of these frameworks — religious instruction and faith

community — can be legitimate ways of doing Christian teaching, but only to the extent that they flow out of the identity of the church or institution in which they are practiced. A seminary or Christian school can legitimately use the religious instruction approach to meet its goals and objectives, but can it also legitimately use the faith community approach? We can readily see that a local church can find a legitimate way of doing Christian teaching through the framework of a faith community; but to what extent can it embrace religious instruction as an authentic way of educating its members?

To be uncritical and unintentional about which framework to build on will lead to a lack of focus and a dissonance between who we are and how we teach. Decide who you are; then decide on how to teach.

Points for Further Thought

- Think about how you go about teaching in your church or school. Does your work setting lean more toward an instruction approach or toward a community approach?

- Can you give an example of how you have used the religious instruction approach in your ministry setting (church or school)?

- Can you give an example of how the faith community approach is practiced in your ministry setting?

- Do you think that your ministry setting can consistently use one framework over the other exclusively? Why or why not?

- Think about your own formative learning experiences. Can you identify which approach has been most influential in your spiritual formation?

Note

1. For a more thorough discussion of other approaches to Christian education, see Jack L. Seymour and Donald E. Miller, *Contemporary Approaches to Christian Education* (Nashville: Abingdon Press, 1982).

Chapter 6

Effective Teaching
for Effectual Faith

A man was out hiking when he fell off a cliff. He managed to grab a thin tree branch sticking out of the side of the rocky cliff wall saving him from plunging thousands of feet below. As his fingers began to slip he prayed fervently to God for deliverance. Suddenly, an angel appeared above, peering over the ledge.

"Who are you?" cried the man.

"I'm an angel. God heard your cry for help. What do you want?" replied the angel.

"Thank heaven!" cried the man. "I want to get off of here!"

"Okay, but I can't do anything if you don't have faith," answered the angel.

"I have faith!" cried the man, "I believe!"

"Do you really believe that God can save you?" asked the angel.

"Yes, I believe!" said the man.

"Okay, then just let go of the branch," replied the angel.

The man paused, and then said, "Is there someone else up there I can talk to?"

As in the case of this desperate fellow, there are things we say we believe and things we really believe — even in matters of faith. How can we know if we really believe something? In order for someone to really believe something, four components (or domains) must be operative to some degree. When all four of the following components are operative, then effectual faith exists:

1. AFFECTIVE (feeling, emotion)

2. COGNITIVE (knowledge, understanding)

3. BEHAVIORAL (action, conduct), and

4. VOLITIONAL (will, conviction, passion)

We can say that a person has an "effectual faith" to the degree that all four components are operative in that person's life. Having an effectual faith means that a person really believes something (whether a value, an idea, a dogma, a doctrine, or an opinion). To the degree that any one of these four key components is not operative in a person's life, then that person does not really believe.

Recently I traveled with someone to a meeting in Washington, D.C. He had offered to pick me up at my office and drive into the city for the meeting. It soon became apparent that though he had offered to drive, he didn't really know the way to our meeting place. Luckily, I was able to give him directions to our destination.

While driving, he explained that, as a rule, when going anywhere he preferred to be the driver and take his own car. He recounted that while a colonel in the armed forces, he became an expert on automobiles. His knowledge included an extensive understanding of automobile design and the results of crashes and accidents. As a result of his experience and knowledge, he announced that he would never ride in a car under a certain weight. On trips he would drive his own car — apparently, even if he didn't know the way and would need to ask someone.

As I listened to him, I thought, "Now here's a person with effectual faith in what he believes." Not only did the colonel have a keen cognitive understanding of automobiles and their design, but he had strong feelings about it. His knowledge, plus his feelings, led to a volitional conviction that was evident in his behavior: he would never drive or ride in cars he knew would not withstand accidents.

When engaging in teaching experiences and relationships, experienced teachers know that they can lead learners through the

AFFECTIVE   COGNITIVE
(heart)   (mind)
                 EFFECTUAL
                    FAITH
BEHAVIORAL   VOLITIONAL
(hands)   (will)

first three domains relatively easily. For example, in the cognitive domain, one can guide a learner through the stages of recall (memorization), comprehension, application, analysis, and evaluation in one single lesson. Likewise, an inspiring teacher can lead his or her students through the stages of the affective domain with success, from receiving to responding to valuing to organization to characterization.

As for changing behavior, any child psychologist (or dog trainer for that matter) will tell you that it's not very difficult. In fact, most behavioral psychologists treating a parent-child conflict are likely to tell you that the problem is not so much a matter of changing the child's behavior as it is changing the parents' behavior. Whenever you teach a learner a new skill, a new method, or a different way of doing something (like tying shoelaces or doing math or driving a car), you are causing change (learning) in the behavioral domain.

But changing behaviors, while relatively easy, can be deceptive. Just because there has been a change of behavior does not mean there has been a change in belief. Again, unless all four components of the affective, cognitive, behavioral, and volitional domains are operative, then there is no real belief, no real effectual faith. In part, this explains why technique-based diets, seminars to quit smoking, or workshops on the spiritual life are ineffective: they tend to focus almost exclusively on the behavioral domain.

Of all the domains, the most difficult in which to do "teaching" is the volitional. More than any other, this is the domain of the Spirit. This is where the deeper relationships are operational. (For example, most people seem not to have learned that the marriage relationship is more a matter of volition than feeling.) Working in this domain, the effective teacher learns to respect the dynamics particular to this domain: relationship, trust, will, honesty, openness, and time. The effective teacher also knows to respect the boundaries over which he or she must not cross. No amount of manipulation or technique can make a learner want or will to learn or to change. That is the prerogative of the individual learner. Learners have the personal freedom to learn or to choose not to learn.

Nevertheless, a shortcoming in much of our teaching in matters of faith is in not addressing matters of volition. Maybe this is because it is the one domain that cannot be taught in one lesson or in the course of one quarter's worth of Sunday school lessons. This is the domain that requires an intentional relationship commitment from the teacher if he or she is to have any meaningful impact in the life of the learner.[1]

Points for Further Thought

- As you examine your aims, goals, and style of teaching, how effective are you in each of the four domains?

- In which domain(s) are you the most effective in your teaching?

- In which domain(s) are you the least effective in your teaching?

- How will you change your teaching to be a more effective teacher for effectual faith in the lives of your learners?

Note

1. This chapter was originally published, in a slightly different form, in *The Sunday School Leader*, July 1997, 7–9. Used by permission. © copyright 1997 The Sunday School Board of the Southern Baptist Convention. All rights reserved.

Chapter 7

Teaching for Obedience

A student in my course on Christian teaching asked to speak with me after class. She had listened politely to the lectures and had participated in all the learning activities during the first few classes. Now, her very apparent frustration with some of her reading material and the course content was getting the best of her. She felt that she needed answers to some pressing questions.

She apologized for her frustration. I told her that was a sure sign she was learning. Dissonance happens when you try to incorporate something new into your existing understanding. With that, she shared her concern. She explained that she was frustrated in teaching because she seemed to see so little change in the lives of her students. She was beginning to wonder if she was a good teacher (in part, that was what had motivated her to take this particular course). She wondered why teaching the Bible and biblical truths seemed to make so little difference. She was feeling ineffective as she saw little change in the lives of her students over the course of months of teaching even the most fundamental and powerful of Christian truths.

Those of us who are teachers can relate to this student's frustrations. We teach week after week (some of us teach year after year) and seem to see so little difference in the lives of our learners. Moments of insight into biblical truths seem not to translate into the living out of those truths in daily living. Children can recite Bible verses from memory but demonstrate no application in their behavior. Youth are bored hearing familiar Bible stories and can name central Christian teachings, yet from Monday to Friday we'd be hard pressed to point out any significant difference between many of them and nonchurched youth. Adults in Sunday school can debate key issues of the Christian life and identify principles for living in the Spirit, yet there is little discernible statistical difference in the divorce rates of nonchurched and church-attending adults. Why does it seem that our efforts at Christian teaching have little effect in the lives of our learners?

I asked my student to engage with the rest of the course from the perspective of discovering a solution to her problem: how to teach students in such a way that there will be change in their lives. She accepted the challenge, and over the next few weeks she approached the learning experiences and the content of the course with that objective in mind.

Several weeks later, my student and I met again to review how her new approach to the course was going. Happily, she had discovered for herself one of the "secrets" to a more effective Christian education: teaching for obedience. She discovered that most learning experiences offered to students in church seem to have more to do with understanding concepts than with applying them. She analyzed that her cerebral approach to teaching about the Christian life was encouraged by an organizational structure that emphasized a "teaching hour" in a "classroom" environment.

Christian teaching is essentially different from any other kind of teaching for the simple reason that at its heart, Christian teaching has more to do with a person — Jesus Christ — than with a body of content. And for that reason, it needs to be taught differently: relationally, not didactically. When Jesus taught as the great Rabbi, as the Master Teacher, he did not open a school for prophets (a seminary) or a college for Pharisees (a law school). Jesus called a group of people together to live with him and learn through the sharing of his personal experience of living and dying during his time on earth. The others who came to hear him teach found that he taught in "a manner like no other." They discovered that he taught them not for knowledge of the Law and the Prophets, but for obedience to God.

Teaching for obedience means teaching for specific changes in the life of the learner. Teaching for obedience requires the following:

- The teacher must already be in obedience to God and to God's teachings. He or she must be intentionally applying the truths of living in obedience to God that he or she is attempting to teach the learners.

- The teacher must communicate the expectation that obedience is the objective of the learning experience (not merely knowledge of the truth or content mastery).

- The teacher must be willing to model obedience for the students.

- The teacher must teach to the objective of obedience: the end result of the teaching experience is that the learner will obey (put into practice) the biblical truth learned.

- The teacher must be willing to hold the student accountable for his or her learning for obedience. Conversely, the teacher must be willing to be held accountable for his or her own commitment to obedience.

- The teacher must be willing to enter the broader domain of the student's life. Learning for obedience does not find ultimate expression in the classroom learning experience, but in the living out of life.

Points for Further Thought

- When you plan your teaching-learning goals and experiences for your learners, are you teaching merely for knowledge and understanding?

- Are you being intentional in teaching for obedience? In what ways?

- Which approach to Bible learning would make a difference in the lives of your learners? Why do you believe so?

- Which approach would make a difference in your life? How so?

Chapter 8

Discovery Learning vs. Expository Teaching

The debate continues as to which are the more legitimate ways of "doing" Christian education. Some say that respect must be given to the content of faith, that *what* we believe is as important as *how* we believe. Others say that schooling models used in traditional church schools are "banking" models that are inappropriate to the spirit of personal freedom that the gospel promises. While most church teachers understand that the use of interactive learning methods is more effective for learning in the domain of the spirit (emotional, volitional, and intuitive), the majority of teachers still seem to lecture for most of the time they are with their learners in church educational functions.

Two competing schools of thought on learning have many implications for Christian education: discovery learning and expository teaching. In this chapter we will examine discovery learning and its implications for Christian teaching. Then we will compare and contrast the claims of David Ausubel's expository teaching along with his critique of discovery learning.

Discovery Learning

Discovery learning can be defined as the learning that takes place when learners are not presented with subject matter in its final form, but rather are required to organize it and discover it for themselves. In this process, learners need to discover the relationships that exist among items of information.

One way to understand the dynamics behind discovery learning is to realize that discovery is really the formation of categories, of coding systems. Categories and coding systems are defined in terms of the relationships (similarities and differences) that exist among objects, concepts, and events. For example, when we ask learners to compare and contrast two ideas or concepts, we facilitate discovery learning.

As a teaching method, the most obvious characteristic of discovery learning is that after the initial stage of the lesson it requires less teacher guidance than do other methods. This does not mean that the teacher ceases to provide any guidance once the problem or project has been presented to the learner. Rather, it implies that the guidance provided will be less directive and that learners will assume more responsibility for their own learning.

Jerome Bruner claims that learners who are regularly exposed to discovery learning approaches benefit from greater transfer of learning, retention, problem solving skills, and motivation.[1] In terms of motivation, he believes that discovery leads to a shift from reliance on external rewards and influences to reliance on intrinsic reinforcement. Since the act of discovery itself is highly pleasant, an external reward is assumed to be unnecessary. Repeated successful discovery experiences make the learner want to learn for the sake of knowing, that is, the more the student learns, the more he or she will want to learn.

There are a number of topics and issues in Christian education that lend themselves to discovery-oriented techniques. Even abstract principles and concepts can be discovered by students in guided discovery situations where sufficient background information and the appropriate experiential methods are provided. Teaching through discovery methods does not imply letting learners go out on their own with no more than the simple instruction, "Go! Discover. . . . " The truth is that the process of discovery itself must be taught through experience as well as through more traditional didactic methods. The learner needs to be guided while in the process of discovering. Used correctly, the teacher's guidance will not ruin the discovery nor destroy its magic.

In *The Process of Education*, Bruner argued for some specific educational practices based on discovery learning that have direct implications for Christian education. For example, as to the question of how young children can learn theological concepts, Bruner would answer that "any subject can be taught to any child in some honest form."[2] Given the perennial debate about how much children really "understand" about belief, conversion, baptism, and other matters of faith, this is quite a statement! While children may not be able to fully comprehend concepts like redemption, propitiation, justice, or sacrifice, these can be reinterpreted and examined in terms of teaching aspects of these concepts appropriate for their age level. Some aspects of forgiveness can be taught to four-year-olds.

The trick, argues Bruner, is to simplify the form and the mode of presentation, gearing it to the simplest representational systems available. For example, since children progress from motor or sensory (enactive) representation to representation in the form of relatively concrete images (iconic), and finally to abstract representation (symbolic), it follows that the sequence of teaching should be the same. For example, a child may not be able to deal with the abstract theological concepts of law and justice, but he or she can relate to policeman and judge as a starting point. A teacher, then, should present a subject so that a child can first experience it, then react to a concrete presentation of it, and, finally, symbolize it.

A second statement by Bruner relevant to Christian education concerns curriculum. He argued that a spiral curriculum that develops and redevelops topics at different grades is ideal for the acquisition of learning.[3] A spiral curriculum that revisits foundational stories and concepts allows for the repetition necessary for learning, for the organization of subject matter in terms of principles, and for the progression from the simplest to the most complex understanding possible. Theoretically, this is highly conducive to the formation of learning structures that in turn facilitate transfer, recall, and discovery. I think of this every time I hear teachers complain, "But they already know this Bible story; they've heard it a hundred times!" That may be true, but hearing the story again, perhaps in a new way, will help learners discover its deeper meanings for their lives today.

In addition, Bruner argued that learners should be taught and encouraged to make guesses.[4] Here Bruner can help inform Christian teachers about intuition, an area often associated with the realm of the spiritual. He believed that to discourage guessing is tantamount to stifling the process of discovery.

Finally, Bruner argues strongly for the use of visual aids. Using audiovisuals provides learners with direct or vicarious experiences and thus facilitates the formation of concepts. This relates directly to Bruner's suggestion that the best instructional sequence is often one that progresses in the same way that the child learning to make sense of the world does — that is, from enactive to iconic and finally to symbolic.[5]

Discovery learning holds some interesting implications for methodology in Christian teaching. Not only does this theory address the question of how learners learn, but it seems to address some of the dynamics of learning often associated with Christian education: intuition, the capacity of children to understand theological concepts, spiral curricula, and the capacity of learners to learn (discover) truths for themselves.

Expository Teaching

As we've seen, discovery learning is an approach to teaching in which the learners are not presented with subject matter in its final form, but rather are required to organize it and "discover" it for themselves. A contrasting school of thought is the expository teaching approach to learning advocated by David Ausubel. He argued that beginning about junior high school age, students can acquire most new concepts and learn new propositions by directly grasping high-order relationships between abstractions. They no longer depend on current or prior concrete-empirical experience for much learning and so are able to bypass completely the intuitive type of understanding that depends on actual experience. Through proper use of expository teaching, learners can proceed directly to a level of abstract understanding that is, according to Ausubel, superior to the intuitive modes of learning. At certain stages of personal development and experience, Ausubel considers it pointless to try to enhance intuitive understanding by using discovery techniques.[6]

One of Ausubel's arguments against discovery learning is that its methods are extremely time-consuming without being a demonstrably superior approach to learning. In addition, Ausubel is probably correct in his observation that most classroom learning derives from some form of expository teaching approach anyway (also called "reception learning" by Ausubel). He argues that meaningful verbal learning occurs mainly in the course of expository teaching. Further, he argues that expository teaching is not passive and does not stifle creativity or encourage mere rote learning.

Like any approach to learning, expository teaching is most effective when used correctly. Ausubel offered some general guidelines for the planning and presentation of subject matter when using expository teaching. For example, as mentioned in chapter 3, the use of an advance organizer is important. An organizer is a complex set of ideas or concepts presented to the learner before the lesson is presented (remember when your teacher used to write "Aim:" on the blackboard before a lesson?). Organizers provide a stable cognitive structure to which the new learning can be anchored in the learner's mind (or "subsumed," to use the technical word).

Another benefit of organizers is their ability to increase recall, or retention. Organizers are most effective when they are used: (1) when learners have no relevant information or experience to which they can relate the new learning you are trying to teach, and (2) when relevant information is already in place, but the learner may not recognize that what he or she already knows is relevant to the new learning. In the first instance, the knowledgeable teacher will use an expository organizer, and in the second instance, the teacher would best use a comparative organizer, making use of similarities and differences between new material and existing knowledge.

Perhaps the most important thing that Ausubel has to say to us as Christian teachers is that the most desirable kind of learning is "meaningful" as opposed to "rote." Here is where he sees the advantage of expository teaching over discovery learning. Meaningfulness refers to the relationship between new learning and existing knowledge. Meaning may be a result of the associations that exist among ideas, events, or objects. But this meaning is not present if the learner is not aware of these associations. A new learning will have meaning only if it relates to a learner's past experience as well as to other ideas and truths being learned at the moment.

What the effective teacher keeps in mind, therefore, is that meaning is not an inherent property of objects or concepts themselves. No idea, concept, or object is meaningful in and of itself; it is meaningful only in relation to the learner. Therefore, the teacher needs to present no new material until the learner is ready in the sense of having appropriate cognitive structure (existing knowledge and experience) to understand it. It is possible, then, that the teacher will need to spend much effort in providing students with background or preliminary information before new learning can take place. But remember, this background or preliminary information can be presented efficiently in the form of advanced organizers. Ausubel contends that after the age of eleven or twelve, most learners have enough background and experience to be able to understand most new concepts very clearly if they are simply explained. Asking a learner to "discover" most concepts is largely a waste of time, he argues.

Research on the relative merits of these two approaches, discovery learning vs. expository teaching, is — you guessed it — inconclusive as to the superiority of one over the other. As Christian teachers, both approaches can serve to inform our work of teaching. When contemplating which teaching approach to use in any given circumstance, the primary question for us should be: For what purpose and for which students and under what learning conditions should we use any one approach over the other? Or is a combination of methods a stronger approach in a given case?

Points for Further Thought

- What are the strengths of using discovery learning in your teaching?

- What are the strengths of using expository teaching as a primary framework for Christian teaching?

- Give an example of how you can use a comparative organizer for your next teaching event.

- Reflect on Jesus' teaching style in the Bible. Do you think he was a "discovery teacher" or an "expository teacher?" Why?

Notes

1. Jerome S. Bruner, "The Act of Discovery," *Harvard Educational Review* (1961): 21–32; *Toward a Theory of Instruction* (Cambridge: Harvard University Press, 1966).

2. Jerome S. Bruner, *The Process of Education* (Cambridge: Harvard University Press, 1961), 52. Copyright © 1960, 1977 by the President and Fellows of Harvard College. Reprinted by permission of Harvard University Press.

3. Ibid.

4. Ibid., 64.

5. Bruner, *Toward a Theory of Instruction,* 49.

6. D. P. Ausubel, *The Psychology of Meaningful Verbal Learning* (New York: Grune & Stratton, 1963), 19.

Chapter 9

Christian Teaching: Values or Content?

Tucked away in one of my educational psychology books is a Peanuts cartoon clipped years ago from a newspaper. It is a cartoon of Peppermint Patty, that endearing character who represents a teacher's worst nightmare: the unmotivated student.

Peanuts

PEANUTS reprinted by permission of United Feature Syndicate, Inc.

Peppermint Patty's sentiment is shared by the educator and therapist Carl Rogers, who stated his belief that, in effect, no one can teach anybody anything.[1] Can that really be true? If so, then why do we expend so much energy, anxiety, and resources in our teaching-learning enterprises? Do we just "carry on" despite the truth?

Carl Rogers decried the meaningless learning experiences that pass for "education." He called for an experiential learning approach that empowered the learner rather than accommodated the teacher. Rogers identified the elements of experiential learning:

- It has a quality of personal involvement.

- It is self-initiated by the student.

- It is pervasive in that it makes a difference in the behavior, attitudes, and personality of the learner.

- It is evaluated by the learner (not the teacher).

- Its essence is meaning.[2]

When it comes right down to it, Christian teaching has more to do with passing on values than with passing on information. In the end, perhaps we should be more concerned about how our students feel about injustice, or how they make value judgments, or what they identify as good, or how they demonstrate love, or how they ascribe worth to themselves as children of God than with how many facts they know, how much information they can retain, or how well they recite biblical content.

But we also realize that values are passed on, in part, through content. Stories of faith, personal stories, and the lessons we choose to teach all pass along values and beliefs. Values are not fostered in a vacuum, and they must be grounded in a critical engagement with foundational beliefs of self, God, the world, right and wrong, good and bad. For Christians, these beliefs are informed by the biblical content.

It may be hard for us to admit, but philosophy, theology, and sound Bible interpretation are exactly what our learners need to help them learn about *how to live!* What philosophers and seers and sages have tried to teach us throughout history is that how you live your life and what you do in life all flow out of your capacity to understand life and self — and understanding life and self is what philosophy and theology are all about. Even children at play struggle to articulate the merits of what is "fair" and why.

So does that mean we should teach our children philosophy and theology? Yes, indeed, children are in a wonderful stage in life during which they are not burdened by operational assumptions about how things work, why things are, or how things ought to be. Unlike adults, who have great difficulty *un*-learning things, children live in a world of constant learning and discovery. What is important to understand here is that good discoverers know how to ask good questions.

This means that our children and youth are able to handle theology. Any time a three-year-old asks, "Why, Mommy?" or a teen asks, "Why me?" they are asking a theological question. The pity is that we're all too quick to give them a mundane answer on the assumption that they can't handle philosophical or theological struggles. They can, and will, if we give them the chance!

Authentic Christian teaching helps children, youth, and adults learn how to ask the right and better questions; it does not give them all the answers. A healthy Christian education creates philosophers and theologians, not human depositories of knowledge and facts.

When it comes to passing on values in Christian education, *how* you teach is as important as *what* you teach. In fact, how you teach may in effect become what you are teaching! Mouthing words of love while giving evidence of prejudice does not teach love, but the lack of it. Here are some suggestions for encouraging values in your teaching-learning experiences:

- List the attitudes and values you wish to encourage.

- Provide learning experiences that will lead to the development of the attitudes and values you want to foster.

- Make use of object lessons. When illustrative incidents occur in the course of events, take advantage of them.

- Apply learning theory. Associate pleasant and positive experiences with the types of behaviors and values you want to encourage.

- Set a good example. Keep in mind the power of identification and imitation of healthy values.

- Keep your personal prejudices under control.

- Remember that the teachers who have the greatest impact in the lives of their learners are those who are secure in what they believe and can share it openly and genuinely.

What are those Christian values worth passing on and demonstrating to your learners? You'll have to work out your own set of values based on your call to teach and on your own goals for teaching, but here are some to consider:

- Love of learning the Bible

- Commitment to regular participation in Christian education (Sunday school, Bible studies, special studies, support groups, etc.)

- Providing a good example of commitment (being on time, participating, intentional affirmation)

- Quality of work

- Teaching for results

- Teaching for obedience to the Word of God

- Genuine love, affection, and respect for learners and fellow teachers

- Respect for the facilities and others' space

- Responsible stewardship of personal gifts and resources

Think of how you go about living out your role as a Christian teacher. Are you passing on the values in your teaching that you want your learners to catch?

Points for Further Thought

- Experiment: focusing on behavior only, what would a first-time visitor learn about Christianity by observing you teach?

- State five personal values you want to teach your learners. Describe ways you can teach those values without "telling" them.

- Do you agree with the statement, "Children learn more by what they see than by what they're told"? If so, provide some examples. How does this apply to Christian teaching?

Notes

1. Carl Rogers, *Freedom to Learn* (Columbus, Ohio: Charles E. Merrill, 1969), 152–53.
2. Ibid., 5.

Chapter 10

Church Life as Curriculum

When I lead educational conferences dealing with curriculum, often I start out by asking the group to share what curriculum they use in their church. Inevitably, participants respond by naming the literature that their teachers and church educators use (usually those provided by the major publishers like Judson Press, Smyth & Helwys, Cokesbury, or David C. Cook — and often some I've never heard of before).

When several in the group have shared, I confess that it was a "trick question," that I had not asked what literature they used but what curriculum they used. I then offer my understanding of what curriculum is: *all those relationships and experiences that are offered to individuals and groups as they participate actively in the life of the congregation.*[1] Once that definition of curriculum is pondered, discussed, and accepted, conversation about curriculum takes on a livelier tone.

Redefining curriculum to mean primarily the life of the church shifts our whole framework for Christian education. This model for Christian teaching in the church offers some significant advantages over other approaches:

- It allows Christian teaching to be informed by the life structure of the church.

- It allows Christian teaching to flow from the church's core identity.

- It respects the rich tradition of the seasons and cycles of the church year.

- It offers limitless possibilities for structuring Christian teaching through the year.

- It helps Christian teaching be more genuine in its programming.

- It helps make for a more natural planning approach to Christian teaching.

- It helps integrate the activity of teaching into the ongoing, cyclical life of the church.

- It makes possible the creation of your own unique curriculum.

The concept of church life as curriculum accepts as true that curriculum is much more than the literature that we choose to use in Sunday morning classes and in study groups. In fact, it is very possible that those who do not attend Sunday school will be more aware of the real curriculum at their church if they are tuned in to the overall church life. Why do I say this? Because anyone who relies heavily on purchased literature and teaching resources is buying a product produced by someone who does not know anything about the uniqueness of your church's life. The learners or teachers who rely heavily on purchased educational literature may base their understanding of their faith more on what a stranger thinks than on what their church believes and lives out.

Publishing houses don't write curriculum for you; they write curricula to sell to as many churches as necessary to make that endeavor a feasible business venture. This is not to discount the quality and validity of curriculum publishers and their ministries. Most do a good service in supplying much-needed resources to churches. But this truth puts a new spin on the understanding of our design, use, and application of curricula in more authentic ways in our local churches.

We said that the church's real curriculum is "all those relationships and experiences that are offered to individuals and groups as they participate actively in the life of the congregation." Let's examine the components of this new definition of curriculum and explore some of its implications.

All Those Relationships...

If there is one truth that separates Christian teaching from other forms of education, it is that in essence Christian teaching is relational. This is because at heart Christian education is not about a creed, or a book, or body of knowledge, but the person Jesus Christ.

It follows, therefore, that while you can strive to comprehend (memorize, study, analyze, master) a book, you cannot "comprehend" a person. To attempt to do so is to objectify the person. The only genuine thing we can do with persons is to be in relationship with them. It's very easy to lose sight of that very essential truth.

We often hear that churches need to incorporate the latest in hi-tech teaching equipment (videos, overhead projectors, computers, "Christian" video games) if they are to succeed in teaching today's learners. But if it's true that authentic Christian education involves the use of "Christian" methodologies, then hi-tech equipment may be the *worst* thing we can introduce into the church learning environment.

Christian education may be the ultimate arena for the "hi-tech vs. hi-touch" paradox in today's society. While we may be tempted to compete with what the community schools have to offer by way of instructional technology, we need to remember that since the nature of Christian education is in essence *relational*, it is inappropriate to compete with schooling methods that are essentially instructional.

Relationships do not translate through video, computer, or hi-tech visuals. Relationships are passed from person to person (hi-touch): always have been; always will be. Hi-tech methods may help or enhance the instructional process, but they can never substitute or make a significant impact on the *kind of learning* that takes place in the higher dimensions of Christian education: being and growing spiritually in relationship with God, self, and others.

If Christian education is to be authentic, then the methods we use in teaching and learning are not didactic ones, but relational ones. The phrase "all those relationships" hints at the significance and place of community in curriculum. Artificial groupings of age-grading and classes will then always be secondary to the power, character, and dynamics of the community at large.

...and Experiences...

Christian educators have long confessed to the detrimental effects of our Western cerebral faith. At its worst Christian education codifies our beliefs to a manageable cognitive exercise of "right belief" at the expense of those other important dimensions of our person: our emotions and will. This tends often to give rise to an adolescent posture that to know the "right answers" is tantamount to having lived them.

The reality, of course, is that God is living, personal, and dynamic. God cannot be contained in mere words, ideas, doctrines, or thought. In the spiritual life the goal is not to comprehend God, but to be consumed by God. If Christian education is to be authentic, then the total person must experience the learning of faith: mentally, emotionally, volitionally, spiritually. Learning will cease to be an exercise of the mind and will become, in effect, the experience of living the life of God in us in its fullest expression according to Jesus' intent: "I am one with them, and you are one with me, so that they may become completely one. Then this world's people will know that you sent me. They will know that you love my followers as much as you love me" (John 17:23, CEV).

...Offered to Individuals and Groups...

Church life as curriculum helps place the focus of Christian education experiences in the context of congregational life, the faith community. Individuals and groups are understood as persons who have in one way or another, at some level, joined with a particular community of faith in significant levels of commitment. The curricula that are offered to individuals and groups flow out of the core community of faith. These are offered with the intent of helping move individuals toward the center of the life of the community. Moving toward the center of community life means greater commitment and investment of self in Christian living.

If Christian teaching is to be authentic, then the curricula offered to individuals and groups within the church will have common overarching goals consistent with the core values and identity of the community. All curricula, for example, will include helping individuals enter into a personal relationship with Jesus Christ and move toward affirming the binding covenant of the faith community. Such curricula will then challenge and enable persons to live out the intent and calling expressed in that covenant.

...as They Participate Actively...

Learning is not a passive activity. Learning is change in a person's behavior, attitudes, and values. Learning in and through relationship calls for active participation in the lives of others within the church and in the world.

If Christian teaching is to be authentic, then it will call learners and teachers to go about their learning, not in a laboratory, but in the arena of life and living. This approach to Christian teaching challenges all to education by discipleship. Successful learning in the Christian life happens in the living and doing, and so curriculum moves out of classrooms and fellowship halls and worship rooms into the mission field of daily living.

...in the Life of the Congregation

At odds with popular cultural notions of individualism is the truth that the Christian life can be lived only in community.

The church is the community that safeguards, calls forth, commissions, equips, and holds to accountability its members. The way a church chooses to structure its living out the calling of God reflects what it values. What is celebrated? What is ignored? Where are most of its energies invested? What is talked about? Who is invited into and sought out for the community? Who is excluded by intent or neglect? On what does the church spend its money? In what proportion?

If Christian education is to be authentic, then it must flow out of and reflect the life of the congregation; it will not be something that is tacked on. Christian teaching will not be delegated to a status of secondary importance; rather, it will be valued and central to the life of the community, highly visible and celebrated.

Points for Further Thought

- What do you like or dislike about the approach to church life as curriculum?

- Do you feel that the idea of church life as curriculum is workable at your church? Why or why not?

- In what ways is church life as curriculum already a reality at your church?

- Is the current Christian education program at your church inconsistent with the ideas of church life as curriculum? In what ways?

- How would taking this model seriously affect the way you do Christian teaching at your church?

Note

1. Adapted from Dennis W. Foust, "Curriculum Engineering in the Local Church: A Contextual Model," Ed.D. dissertation, Southern Baptist Theological Seminary, 1988, 8. Used by permission.

Chapter 11

Worship as Christian Education

As I speak with ministers and church educators around the country, I continue to be surprised by current ideas and notions of Christian teaching in churches. Despite years of struggling and "preaching" by educators to liberate Christian education from dated models inconsistent with the nature of Christian discipleship, education continues to be relegated to a secondary status in many churches. In fact, one church observer noted that, for many, worship is seen as necessary, while educational and learning activities are seen as highly optional in the Christian life.[1]

This flies in the face of evidence to the contrary. In 1990, the Search Institute concluded a three-and-a-half year national study of effective Christian education in Protestant congregations. The most remarkable finding of that study was that there are only two significant factors that make a difference in helping persons attain a mature faith. One of them is the amount of exposure and participation in Christian education![2] It's not the size of a church, the denominational affiliation, the level of education, or the particular worship style — only participation in effective Christian education makes a difference in attaining a mature faith.

When asked about the place of Christian teaching in the local church, I eventually find myself emphasizing two things: (1) everything we do is Christian education, and (2) the best educational experience we provide is when we gather for corporate worship. I continue to be amused at how novel and foreign this second point seems to be to most pastors and educators I talk to. For many, programs modeled on schooling, like Sunday school and Bible study groups, are the primary educational

functions of their churches. The perception is that if it doesn't happen in a classroom, "it ain't education."

I am convinced that some of the best and most effective Christian teaching we do happens in our corporate worship experience. This is not a novel idea; Christian education in the primitive church was worship-centered and liturgically based. During the centuries of mass illiteracy that followed, the church educated its people through the corporate worship experience. The oral tradition was passed on through proclamation, the written word was preserved in the texts, the gospel stories were depicted on stained-glass windows and icons. The drama of the Mass taught in the most powerful ways the spiritual reality of the Word made flesh.

In Chapter 5 we argued that effectual faith has four operative components: affective (the heart of faith), cognitive (the mind of faith), behavioral (the hands of faith), and volitional (the soul of faith). The power of corporate worship as Christian education is the incorporation of all of those dimensions in the central and binding experience of the church.

Worship as an authentic Christian teaching approach has a long history in the life of the church. The unique nature of Christian teaching requires attention to the whole person: body, mind, soul, and spirit. In terms of teaching for an effectual faith, the corporate worship experience addresses all of the pertinent personal components: cognitive, affective, behavioral, and volitional. To the extent that each of these components is operative, a person can be said to have an effectual faith. That measure is the extent to which a person "believes" and lives consistently out of his or her faith.

Cognitive: The cognitive domain relates to ideas, knowledge, understanding, and comprehension. The parts of the worship experience that connect with this component include preaching, readings, prayers, children's sermons, hymn texts, the church year emphases and themes, attention to Christian traditions, and the intentional proclamation of our corporate identity.

Affective: The affective domain deals with feelings and emotions. Components of worship that educate our emotions are music, memories, fellowship, the moving of the Spirit, ambiance (the feeling and mood provided by candles, space, banners, symbols), drama and dance, prayers, feeling connected and loving toward the people of God, and feeling loved by God and others.

Behavioral: The behavioral domain is expressed in action and conduct. Though not necessarily overtly observed, thinking also is a behavior. Several parts of the worship experience are behavioral: movement (processing, posture, kneeling), offerings, expressions of worship and praise, participation, and prayers. Thoughtful engagement in the dialogue of the sermon is an action, and the call for a personal or corporate response at the end of the service is an intentional connection to the behavioral domain.

Volitional: The domain we call volition has to do with passion, will, and conviction. Corporate worship is an expression of the spirit of belief, but at times it is necessary for us to exercise our faith in the midst of doubt, pain, and distant, unrealized hope.

•

Choosing to worship is an existential experience. No one worships without personally choosing to do so. Worship doesn't just happen — even for the teenager who is at church only because his or her parents insist on it.

But if you doubt that even passive participation in worship has some didactic benefit, let me share a recent experience. In preparation for our Children's Sunday worship celebration, the Wednesday night children's program that week was on corporate worship. At one point in the lesson the children were asked

Educational Components of Corporate Worship

	Worship Service Components	Teaching Dynamics
COGNITIVE	Readings Preaching Hymn texts Bible text Listening Prayers Worship bulletins	Knowledge and comprehension of the *content* of one's faith is important and foundational. Most people learn their theology through hymns and the core biblical story through preaching.
AFFECTIVE	Music Hymns Symbols Ambiance Rituals Colors Banners Sermon illustrations	The affective domain addresses the emotional way of learning and knowing. This may be the door to the volitional component of an effectual faith.
BEHAVIORAL	Movement Cultural practices Dance Confessions Posture Prayers	Kinesthetic learning is one of the most powerful learning modes we have. It touches on memory and experience. Behaviors help connect ideas with external reality.
VOLITIONAL	Existential participation Call to Response Baptism Lord's Supper Fellowship Celebration Praise Confession	The final domain of the Spirit is in our wills or souls. Learning happens when there is a change in the learner in behavior, knowledge, attitude, or belief. Conversion is the ultimate form of learning, for it is the ultimate form of change.

to name as many parts of the worship service they could remember. Much to my amazement, they named them all! And they named them correctly, identified where in the service they happened, and could tell me the purpose they served in the worship experience.

Then I asked, "What about the 'B' word?" After some puzzled looks, one of them said, "Oh, you mean boring!"

"Yes," I said. "I always hear kids say church is boring. Why do you think that's so?"

"Because it's not for kids," one replied.

"Because it's for big people," said another.

They all agreed that the church service was boring, but then one of them said, "Yes, but if you really pay attention, it's really interesting!"

Well, that one just about floored me! Not only did one of them confess that corporate worship can be interesting, even for children, but by virtue of being able to name every component of the worship service they demonstrated that they were getting a lot of good Christian education in their worship experience.

Because the nature of the Christian faith is more a matter of claiming the heart and will than it is a matter of filling the mind (knowing, understanding, comprehending), the way we do Christian teaching must be consistent with that end. And don't doubt that Christian discipleship has always been a matter of the will. Jesus' call to his disciples was to follow and believe, not to study or attend a seminar. Their belief in Jesus was the result of experiencing God through him and in knowing through the words and works of God. The teaching method of choice was being in personal relationship with the Son of God, not learning how to argue the finer points of the Law.

Instruction, training, and educational models do have their place in Christian education. And most of our teachers teach well; some are, in fact, masterful at their craft. But to concentrate solely on schooling approaches in the Christian teaching of our members will result in a lack of spiritual depth. While the Sunday school hour is just as important for Christian education as other educational opportunities in the church, it is arguable that it is not the most important.

This is not to denigrate the significant, life-changing work Sunday school teachers do. It is indispensable! Neither does that statement discount the significance of the Sunday morning educational program; even the more "traditional" Sunday schools do good service. But let's face it, there are several limitations inherent in the Sunday school classroom approach to Christian teaching:

- It is based on a schooling model often at odds with the dynamics, nature, and reality of the Christian faith.

- Actual "instructional time" amounts to at most 40 minutes on a good Sunday morning. (That's 40 *minutes* a *week* for religious instruction, or about 34 hours a year. Compare that with the 5 hours a day of TV the average American child watches, which adds up to 1,825 hours a year! And yes, they are learning while they watch TV, unfortunately.)

- Quality assurance is difficult due to limited resources, limited or wasted space, and the dependence on volunteers as teachers (and thank God for each one of them!).

- While frustration with prepackaged standardized curricula is perennial, so is the dependence on the publishing houses' ideas of Christian education's nature, philosophy, function, goals, and methods.

This is not an argument to do away with the Sunday school. We need it! This is an invitation to *widen our definition* of Christian education in the church. In doing so, we can then intentionally go about effectively identifying and shaping dimensions of Christian education other than instruction: mentoring, nurture, modeling, guiding, formation. We'll begin to explore Christian education outside the classroom setting: outdoors in nature, on retreat, in homes, on the streets, on stage, in *other* classrooms, in cyberspace, at play, at work, through the arts, through spiritual disciplines of mind, soul, and body, and many others. And we'll be forced to use new and more experiential methods to process these dimensions of Christian education: dance, meditation, readings, drama, deeper dialogues, contemplation, the arts, creative prayer, vocation, community, research, and many more yet to be discovered and applied.

In sum, if I were forced to say when the single most important educational experience in the life of the church takes place, I'd probably say, "During the worship hour." Done well, it is the single most significant educational event in the average church week. A blend of tradition and innovation in music and word, form and content, holds us in tension between the past that shaped us and the future that calls to us. The worship room is an explosion of symbols in color, form, design, sound, light. There are music, space, banners, words, objects, and movement all constantly teaching at many levels: visual, auditory, emotional, didactical, and, certainly, spiritual. And it all happens, not in a classroom, but in an authentic context of the Christian faith: the community gathered.

I think that's an excellent expression of Christian education at its best. As with all other functions of the church, like stewardship, mission, and witness, a legitimate Christian education flows out of worship, the starting point for all of the church's functions, because worship in essence is the confession that "God is God, and we are God's people."

Points for Further Thought

- Can you identify some overt educational components in your church's worship service?

- The author contends that some of the best Christian teaching happens during corporate worship. Do you agree with that statement? Why or why not?

- If someone new to your church participated in your worship service, what would they "learn" about what your church believes about God? About people? About the world?

- If your church had no educational opportunities other than Sunday morning worship, what would you have to change, add, supplement, or substitute in the worship service to ensure the best Christian teaching for your congregation?

Notes

1. *Master Notes: Stewardship Resources for Church Leaders* 4, no. 2 (1995).

2. Peter L. Benson and Carolyn H. Elkin, *Effective Christian Education: A National Study of Protestant Congregations — A Summary Report on Faith, Loyalty and Congregational Life* (Minneapolis: Search Institute, 1990).

Part 3

The Teacher

Chapter 12

The Spiritual Roles of the Christian Teacher

Teaching is one of the primary callings in the church, both in importance and necessity. In the early church, the function and calling of teaching was indistinguishable from that of pastor. But in our age of specialization, teaching has come to stand alone as a distinct calling in the church that includes both professional and lay educators.

The spiritual role and calling of teacher in the church is unique. In fact, the challenge of being a Christian teacher is such that James the apostle warned, "My friends, not many of you should become teachers. As you know, we teachers will be judged with greater strictness than others" (James 3:1, TEV). That may not be the most motivational verse in the Bible, but it does affirm the significance of the craft of Christian teaching. Because of the nature of the setting in which Christian education takes place — the church, the Body of Christ — the function of teaching takes on dimensions not found in other arenas. Functioning as a teacher in a college classroom or in an elementary school or even in a seminary graduate course is different from practicing the role of a teacher in the church setting.

Assumptions

Three underlying assumptions about Christian teaching in the church provide the basis for understanding the spiritual roles of the Christian teacher.

1. The Holy Spirit is active in the teacher-learner relationship. Unique to Christian teaching is the enabling partnership of the Holy Spirit. Unlike other teacher-learner relationships, in Christian education the Spirit enables a more reciprocal dynamic in learning experiences. The Spirit is there to guide and teach both the teacher and the learner.

2. Christian learning is a lifelong process. Since the Christian's calling is "to become" and to "grow up into Him who is the head," Christian teaching is a critical component to growth in the spiritual life. No one graduates from Sunday school. We don't give out master's degrees in the Christian life. Once a Christian sets his or her foot on the path of discipleship the journey never ends.

3. Christian teaching is uniquely different from other ways of teaching. Christian education has more to do with matters of the spirit and will than of the mind. We've argued that the content of Christian education is not a body of knowledge, but a person: Jesus Christ. Knowing God is primary in Christian teaching; knowing *about* God is secondary. Therefore, basic educational categories in Christian teaching (content, the role of the teacher, the role of the student, methodology, epistemology, etc.) take on a distinct quality.

To argue that the role of the teacher in Christian education is more "spiritual" is not to say that it makes for an easier task. Below I discuss five roles that Christian teachers must master to become effective in working out their calling.

Content Specialist

The Christian teacher must be in a growing personal relationship with Jesus Christ. Note that we avoid saying that the teacher must "know" Jesus in order to avoid the temptation to objectify a person. Being in relationship with a person is different from "knowing" a book or mastering content. To the extent that one's relationship with the living Christ is real and dynamic and operative, to that extent one can be an effective Christian teacher.

Secondarily to that relationship with Christ, the teacher will be effective to the extent that he or she has mastered the content of the faith: history, the biblical literature, classic spiritual writings, theology, doctrine, and Christian arts. Some may argue, "But I only teach preschoolers; I don't need to know all that!" Or, "I teach youth. They'd be bored to tears if I talked about theology or history."

The fact is that in the business of lifelong Christian discipleship, all of these matter. The greatest tragedies in the history of the church have been aided in part by ignorance of sound theology, lack of knowledge of history, biblical illiteracy, and an inability to appreciate the awakening and inspiring powers of the arts. These are necessary even from the earliest years when children are beginning to learn to order and understand their world. For the adolescent, exposure to history, the arts, and theology is a helpful cure for the egocentricity that is normative for that age group.

Instructor

Instruction refers to the art and technique of teaching. The Christian teacher must be both artist and technician when it comes to the learning arts. Leon McKenzie said, "A false mysticism which maintains that the good intentions of the religious educator are alone important, and that the Holy Spirit will intervene to salvage poor instruction, is perhaps the primary source for ineffectual instruction."[1]

The spiritual role of instructor includes mundane matters such as classroom management, formulating learning outcomes, sequencing activities, and operating an overhead projector. But instruction also includes loftier skills like motivating the learner, firing the imagination, and inspiring action and application of biblical truths to daily living.

Counselor

One of the most natural roles of the teacher is that of counselor. It will not take long for learners to seek out good teachers for advice and counsel. The spiritual role of counseling is much more than helping with decision-making, listening, and giving advice. The teacher must be able to help learners explore their life situations and help them discover their own paths in Christian discipleship.

But counseling requires more than good intentions. The teacher will need skills, understanding, and expertise that come only through study and experience. The Christian teacher must be knowledgeable about counseling theory, models, and their appropriate use in the Christian education setting of the teacher-learner relationship.

Model and Mentor

Perhaps the spiritual role that is most demanding of the Christian teacher is that of being a model and mentor to learners. Being a model in the Christian life is a daunting prospect, because we realize that this comes not out of performance, but out of being. We are called to be teachers not because we perform well in a classroom, but because we live a Christian life based on our relationship with Jesus Christ. It is in the being and the relationship that we model all else. How much we know, how well we teach, is secondary and consequential.

The spiritual role of the mentoring relationship perhaps is the highest expression of Christian teaching. When a teacher and a learner enter into this relationship, a new dimension of learning takes place. A higher level of mutual responsibility and accountability exists in this teaching-learning relationship. In the spiritual role of mentor, teachers share more than skills and knowledge; they share the passion of their calling, dreams, visions, and hopes.

Learner

The most fundamental role of the teacher, however, may be that of learner. Only the teacher that is growing and learning will serve learners well. The calling to be a teacher is not for those who have "arrived"; it is for those who can model in their lives and living what it means to be a lifelong disciple of Jesus Christ; ever growing, ever learning, ever becoming — that is perhaps the greatest lesson one can teach.

As you seek to grow in your calling as a teacher, give attention to the spiritual roles of teaching. Take a moment to articulate your assumptions about your roles in teaching and learning.

Points for Further Thought

- At which of the spiritual roles are you most competent: content expert, instructor, counselor, model and mentor, or learner?

- How is each spiritual role evident in your teaching ministry?

- How can you become better in the spiritual role in which you are lacking?

Note

1. Leon McKenzie, "Developmental Spirituality and the Religious Educator," in *The Spirituality of the Religious Educator*, ed. James Michael Lee (Birmingham: Religious Education Press, 1985), 63. Used by permission of the publisher, Religious Education Press, 5316 Meadow Brook Road, Birmingham, Alabama, U.S.A.

Chapter 13

How to Become
a *Very* Good Teacher

At a recent workshop for teachers and church leaders, I asked the participants to introduce themselves before we got down to the business of learning. Participants were to introduce themselves by stating their name, what church they were from, what they did there, and why they chose to attend this particular workshop.

One person's response to this icebreaker exercise caught me by surprise. So much so, that I've been thinking about it ever since. When her turn came, a woman introduced herself as Joyce, named the church where she served as a youth teacher, and then said, "I chose this workshop because I want to learn how to become a *very* good teacher."

Well, that certainly was the right attitude! I wasn't sure if the workshop content would definitely help her in learning how to become a *very* good teacher. But hearing her state that as her goal, I knew she was on the way to becoming just that.

Becoming a very good teacher does not happen by chance or happenstance. In fact, becoming a very good anything doesn't "just happen." To become very good at something requires dedication and discipline. One characteristic of persons who are very good at what they do is that they know certain things that others do not, and know them well. Here I discuss six things you'll need to know if you want to become a *very* good teacher.

Know the Theory

I know, "theory" sounds boring, but I know of very few people who are very good at what they do who are not at least familiar with the theories underlying their profession, avocation, or craft. Theories of learning describe and explain for us the conditions under which learning does and does not occur (for example, how do you know your student has really "learned"?).

Here's a definition: "A theory of learning is a general concept which applies to all organisms, to all learning tasks, and to all situations where learning occurs. It considers the conditions which give rise to learning as the cause, and the learning itself as the effect."[1] (I warned you this part was boring.)

Theories of learning and teaching are important because they give us the "big picture." They help explain why things work and why they don't, how things fit together and how they shouldn't. Knowing learning theory and knowing the names and basic ideas of important theorists (like Piaget, Erikson, Ausubel, Bandura, Bloom, Groome, Edge, McKenzie, R. C. Miller, Kohlberg, Westerhoff, Gagné, Gessell, Thorndike, and Montessori) will give your teaching a sound grounding. Very good teachers know theory.

Know the Craft

Theory is important, but theory alone will not carry you in the learning environment. Two- and three-year-olds don't respond well to conversations about theory. But let's be realistic: most adults don't respond well to conversations about theory either.

There's nothing quite like watching a master craftsperson at work. A teacher who is good at the craft inspires learning. The craft of teaching includes knowing how to ask questions, how to motivate students, how to use educational technologies, how to lead a dialogue, how to prepare audiovisuals, how to "read" a group, how to plan a lesson, how to discipline and how to give praise, and how to model behavior and attitudes. And it includes knowing when to speak and when not to speak, when to give a little and when to push, even how to wipe a runny nose and how to keep chalk dust off your dark blue suit.

Know the Content

How you teach is, of course, just as important as *what* you teach. But lately, the teaching profession seems to have fallen into the trap of worrying more about style than about content. That's a subtle temptation, and sometimes it's hard to discern the difference because often in teaching "the medium is the message." This certainly is true in Christian teaching, where the teacher is the medium of the message of God's love.

Knowing the content of your teaching is critical. What do you believe? What is right and good and true? One of the worst sins a Christian teacher can commit is not knowing the content of our faith: the Bible. We all dread having our children wind up under a teacher like the one who gave this lecture on the Prodigal Son to her students:

"All right, class," the teacher said. "There was a man of the Pharisees named Nicodemus who went to Jericho by night. And he fell upon stony ground and the thorns choked him half to death.

"The next morning Solomon and his wife, Gomorrah, came by and they took him down to the ark so that Moses could care for him. But as he was going through the eastern gate toward the ark, his hair was caught in a limb, and he hung there forty days and forty nights. Afterward he was hungry and the ravens came and fed him.

"The next day three wise men came and carried him down to the boat dock, where he caught a ship to Nineveh. When he got there, he saw Delilah sitting on a wall.

"And Nicodemus said, 'Throw her down off the wall.' And the wise men said, 'How many times shall we throw her down? Seven times seven?' And Nicodemus replied, 'Nay, but seventy times seven.' And they threw her down 490 times. She burst asunder in their midst, and they picked up twelve baskets of fragments. My question is: 'Whose wife will she be in the resurrection?' "[2]

In terms of biblical illiteracy among teachers, I haven't seen anything that bad, but some have come close! Know your content!

Know the Goal

Christian teaching doesn't happen in a vacuum. Like the gospel, it comes always in context and relationships. The gospel will take on the characteristics of what it looks like, how it behaves, and what it does depending on the context in which it is incarnate. And the gospel will find its face, its hands, and its speech through the relationships within that context. Authentic Christian teaching takes seriously the context and relationships out of which it flows.

Only when Christian teaching flows out of the context and relationships can the important questions of intent be answered. To what end are you teaching? How will you know when your teaching ministry has produced fruit? The classic understanding of Christian teaching is to help believers become more Christ-like. Having that as your goal will help you make decisions about both content and methodology: What will you need to teach to help your students become more Christ-like? How will you need to teach to help your students become more Christ-like?

Knowing the context of your teaching and shaping the relationships that flow out of the context of teaching will define your goals.

Know the Student

Some teachers see students as containers to be filled; others see them as lamps to be lit. How you understand your students will determine how you treat and teach them. Knowing the student includes understanding how individual students learn. There are over twenty-five distinct learning styles, and research on multiple intelligences that impact on the teaching-learning process are just beginning to be explored.[3]

Learners are not blank slates when they enter the learning environment. Neither are they finished products; they are persons in process — each in the middle of the story of redemption being written on the tablet of their lives. Effective teachers find ways to intersect in the lives of their learners at whatever point of the story they find themselves.

Know Yourself

Finally, the best teachers, the very good teachers, are those who know themselves. That is a sign of someone who has been a good student of others, life, and self. In the end, the best you will ever offer your students will not be how much you know, how smart you are, or how well you teach. The very best teachers are those who are able to give of themselves and teach their students in the classroom of life.

Points for Further Thought

- Are you willing to do what it takes to become a very good teacher? Why?

- Describe in one paragraph your idea of "the big picture" of the purpose of Christian teaching in your church or ministry setting.

- What are the most useful skills you have as a teacher? Did these come naturally to you or did you have to develop them?

- Have you memorized the list of all the books in the Bible? Do you think that would be helpful? Why or why not?

- Do you know your learning style preference? If not, how would you describe your teaching style?

- Can you state your "Credo" — what you believe? Can you give a reason for what you believe?

Notes

1. John P. DeCecco and William R. Crawford, *The Psychology of Learning and Instruction: Educational Psychology,* 2d ed. (Englewood Cliffs, N.J.: Prentice-Hall, 1968), 5.

2. Downloaded from the Ecunet information service, Online Service Company, Lawrenceville, Ga.

3. See the works of Howard Gardner, *Frames of Mind, Multiple Intelligences: The Theory in Practice* (New York: Basic Books, 1983); and *The Unschooled Mind: How Children Think and How Schools Should Teach* (New York: Basic Books, 1991).

Chapter 14

Learner Needs and Teacher Skills

Every now and again I find myself in a seminar or workshop where the leader will ask the question, "Who is the teacher who had the most influence on you?" or, "Which teacher do you remember best, and why?"

This question usually is followed by an exercise in identifying the characteristics of an influential or effective teacher. While the exercise is meant to focus on the teacher, a close look at any list of effective teacher characteristics will reveal something interesting: they all directly relate to the needs of the learner.

Effective teachers understand the needs of the learner and can adapt their personal teaching style to meet those needs. Your group of learners will have particular and individual needs you have to be aware of. But in one sense, all learners share some basic needs when it comes to the teaching-learning relationship. Here I consider five universal learner needs.

To Have a Conducive Learning Environment

We may think of learning as an activity of the mind, but really we are built to learn with our whole selves, including our bodies. In fact, our primary way of knowing is through our senses — through what we see, feel, and hear. The environment in which we find ourselves can either help or hinder learning.

I recently led a conference that had two separate sessions, one in the morning and one in the afternoon. The morning crowd was alert, chipper, attentive and participated in the discussion of the content. The afternoon learners, however, shuffled in after a long lunch to a very warm room (the A/C seemed to be dragging too). The deadly combination of full stomachs, afternoon hours, and stuffy room caused the learning curve to take a nosedive!

Effective teachers will strive to provide a safe, stimulating environment appropriate to the developmental stage of their learners. Children need a consistent, warm, and welcoming environment. Teens may learn best in a wacky setting with constant stimulation, while adults need comfort to learn best.

To Receive Accurate Information

Receiving accurate information leads to trust on the part of the learner. Nothing is more insulting to a learner than the feeling that a teacher has not taken the time to prepare. And nothing is more devastating to the teacher-learner relationship than the suspicion on the part of the learner that the teacher doesn't know what he or she is talking about.

Not too long ago, our youngest son came home saying he didn't want to take music at school anymore. When asked why, he replied that his teacher didn't know anything about music. Well, that kind of remark calls for an investigation. It turned out that our son had learned the correct way of breathing and singing from his church choir teacher (a professional singer). When he started getting "wrong" instructions from his school music teacher on singing technique, he lost all confidence in her ability to teach him anything.

Effective teachers do their homework. Be a good learner first in order to be a good teacher. Know your stuff!

To Receive Relevant Information

One of the most frustrating — though appropriate — questions that learners (especially teenage learners with an attitude) ask is "So what?" Few of us can handle "learning for the future" effectively. Phrases like, "This will come in handy some day," or "Some day you'll understand what I'm talking about," translate to "I really don't need to pay attention to this stuff" in the mind of the learner.

Effective teachers teach to meet the life needs of their learners. Unless the content of your teaching relates to the immediate life circumstances of the learner, you may be engaged in nothing greater than a glorified game of Trivial Pursuit. Think about it this way: what difference will it make in your learners' lives that you taught them today?

To Be Challenged to Learn

When I was a school principal, I once took a chance in hiring an inexperienced teacher for a first-grade class — a very critical grade for children. Her degree wasn't in elementary education, and she had no experience with either the curriculum or in teaching. But she had one quality that neither years of classroom experience nor a college education can give: enthusiasm. If there's one thing a first-grader needs above anything else, it's an enthusiastic teacher willing to do whatever it takes for her students to learn. By the end of the year, her class led the other four first-grade classes in its reading level on standardized tests (not to mention in enthusiasm).

Effective teachers communicate enthusiasm and expectations for learning. They ask prompting questions. They issue challenges to learning, like "I'm going to ask a difficult question now, but I think you'll be able to get the answer if you think about it a little." Remember, learners will rise to your level of expectation.

To Feel Loved and Valued

Learning may be a matter of the mind, but Christian education is also a matter of the heart. If you're a parent, you learned very early on that your children really never cared about how smart you are. Their chief concern in their relationship with you has always been "Do you love me?" It's the same in the teacher-learner relationship. You can impress your learners with your mastery of content and your vast mental storehouse of biblical trivia, but in the end your learners just need to know that you love them.

Effective teachers express their concern and love for learners. They contact them outside the learning environment: they send a card, make a phone call, acknowledge and celebrate their accomplishments. One of the teachers I remember most is Mr. Paris, my high school history teacher. I don't remember much of the history that Mr. Paris taught; I remember him and his class for something else. Whenever I would enter his classroom with my art portfolio under my arm, Mr. Paris would insist on having me show my artwork to the class. It always astounded me that a history teacher would take five minutes out of his class time for an aspiring artist to show off his work — after all, what does history have to do with art, right? Mr. Paris never insisted on an academic tit-for-tat from me, no hint of any expectation that I should pay closer attention in class, or that I do better on exams, or even that I be more enthusiastic about the subject that was close to his heart.

I didn't learn much history in Mr. Paris's class (more a comment on my study habits than on his teaching ability, to be sure), but I learned the power of a teacher taking a personal interest in his students on their own terms.

Giving attention to these universal learner needs in your teaching will help ensure that your name will be the one mentioned when one day a student of yours is asked, "Who is the teacher who most influenced you?" Mr. Paris is on my top ten list.

Points for Further Thought

- Who is the teacher who had the most significant influence on you? How so?

- In what ways do you try to provide a positive learning environment for your learners?

- How many hours a week do you spend preparing for your teaching experiences? Is this adequate enough to make you feel confident?

- Are you satisfied that what you are teaching your learners is relevant to their lives? If not, then why are you teaching so?

- In your teaching, do you challenge your learners? In what ways?

- Can you name ways you show love toward your learners? Do you take an interest in their personal lives?

- Examine the chart of Categories of Effective Teacher Skills on the facing page. Identify those in which you excel. Identify those in which you need improvement. What are some ways you can improve in your areas of need?

CATEGORIES OF EFFECTIVE TEACHER SKILLS

Classroom management

- Creating a learning environment
- Handling learner behaviors
- Optimizing instructional time

Personal time management

- Prioritizing for personal learning
- Practicing spiritual disciplines
- Continuing education training
- Getting in and out of the classroom on time

The art of teaching (the inspiration)

- Motivating learners for learning
- Creating lifelong learners
- Teaching for application and obedience

The science of teaching (the technique)

- Making and using audiovisuals and media
- Using effective and dramatic storytelling
- Mapping a lesson plan

Hermeneutics ("rightly dividing the Word of God")

- Understanding biblical chronology
- Knowing biblical geography
- Correctly interpreting a passage of Scripture

Chapter 15

Planning the Teaching Experience

I had two fine theology professors in seminary, each with a distinctive teaching style at opposite ends of the didactic spectrum. One professor was meticulous, logical, focused, and controlled. He taught from lecture notes outlined on the overhead projector and you could follow his arguments and reasoning as he scanned down the screen, line upon line, precept upon precept. In fact, you could follow along in your own unauthorized copy of his lecture notes available for a modest price from an enterprising former student. The outline never varied.

My other theology professor couldn't be more different. Rather than tell you about theology, he "did theology" in class. His presentations were rambling, spontaneous, and dynamic, which made for great class sessions, but what a time we had preparing for a test! This teacher was at his best when he lost control of his teaching.

When I first started teaching, I planned everything. It helped me feel confident knowing that I was going to be in control of the learning process. But eventually I discovered that I was at my best when I learned to lose control of my teaching. Planning does benefit teacher and learners, and a good teacher is always prepared, but in the end, teaching is more of an art than a science. As we've said, Christian teaching is more a matter of the spirit than of the mind, of volition than of certitude.

Research into teacher planning yielded some interesting findings. While planning does help teachers carry out their instructional plan in the classroom, it functions primarily for the benefit of the teacher. Lesson planning is a means of organizing instruction and gives the psychological benefit of helping the teacher feel confident, secure, and in control.[1]

But findings indicated that planning which leads to a teacher-controlled session in some cases has adverse effects on learning. In one research study, more teacher planning correlated with: (1) poorer student achievement, (2) poorer student attitude toward the teacher, subject matter, and instructional mode, and (3) poorer attitude toward the students on the part of the teacher.[2]

Another researcher concluded that objectives-first models of planning decrease the teacher's sensitivity to the ideas, thoughts, and actions of the learners. It was discovered that while most planning statements had an effect on the classroom behavior of the teacher, there was little correlation between such statements and dealing with the learners' needs.[3]

The studies found that in the lesson planning process, many good teachers prepared their written plans in the form of an outline, which served as a memory jogger to keep them on course. The major part of planning remained a mental process that never got written down. It seems good teachers leave room for the unpredictable and learn to incorporate it into the learning experience.

Before you throw away your Sunday school teaching guide in jubilation and anticipation of free Saturday evenings from now on (yes, we know when you plan your lessons!), remember the following:

- Good planning does have important benefits for you, the teacher, as well as for your learners.

- Teaching may be more art than science, but artists also must be disciplined, and success comes only from practice, practice, practice.

- To increase lesson relevance, begin your planning with your students' needs in mind first; then formulate your teaching objectives.

- Christian teaching primarily is relational, not didactic. Leave room for the Spirit to teach through you and your students.

- Finally, goals and objectives still are important: if you aim at nothing, you are bound to hit it. But the real content of Christian teaching is our relationship with God — and in that matter, we know who should be in control.[4]

Points for Further Thought

- When you plan your lessons, do you focus more on your performance or on the needs of your learners?

- As a rule, do you overprepare or do your underprepare for teaching a lesson? Is this intentional? What is the result?

- What is the one teaching skill you need most to practice? What might happen if you got very good at that skill?

- How significant are the relational dynamics between you and your learners in your teaching? Do you get "below the surface" of the teacher-learner relationship?

Notes

1. C. M. Clark and R. J. Yinger, *Three Studies of Teacher Planning*, Institute for Research on Teaching, Research Series No. 55 (East Lansing, Mich.: Michigan State University, 1979).

2. E. W. Eisner, "Educational Objectives: Help or Hindrance?" *School Review* 75 (Autumn 1967): 250–66.

3. G. McCutcheon, "How Do Elementary School Teachers Plan Their Courses?" *Elementary School Journal* 81 (1980): 4–23; P. L. Peterson, et al., "Teacher Planning, Teacher Behavior, and Student Achievement," *American Educational Research Journal* 15 (1978): 417–32.

4. This chapter was previously published in a slightly different form in *Compass: Ministry Tools for Shaping Lives* 1, no. 6 (September 1995): 3. Used by permission of Smyth & Helwys Publishing, Inc.

Part 4

The Craft

Chapter 16

Adding Motivation in Your Teaching

Here's the bad news: the truth is, we can't teach anybody anything.

The good news, however, is that people *learn*. We can't teach a truth — or even a simple fact — to someone who is not ready to learn. It's like trying to teach a pig to sing: it just wastes your time and annoys the pig. Good teachers facilitate learning. *Great* teachers know how to motivate and inspire learning in others.

Still, motivating learners is one of the most difficult challenges for teachers. As any experienced teacher knows, attempts at motivating learners to *want* to learn often degenerate to ... well, there's no nice way to put it: bribes! And those soon lose their effectiveness (really, how long can you "up the ante" with what you use to bribe learners?). You know you're in trouble when your primary motivational method is "If you don't pay attention I'll...."

Good teachers know that the best motivation is an internal desire to learn and participate. External motivators tend to be little more than "attention getters." True motivations are based on perceived personal needs, real or imagined.

Lawrence O. Richards, in his classic book *Creative Bible Teaching,* pointed out that while teachers understand the personal factors of motivation, they often neglect what he called the "structural factors in motivation." Structural factors are those elements that are built into the structure of the lesson. Understanding and using these structural factors in your teaching will help you plan lessons that motivate your learners to learn. Here are four factors of motivation you can incorporate into your lesson structure.

Learners Learn Best
When the Learning Is Patterned

A patterned learning experience is one in which the learner recognizes a goal and can see progress toward it. This approach sets a goal that has meaning for the learners, giving them a stake in the lesson. Learners are motivated to participate because achieving the goal will meet their needs or wants.

You can have a hidden purpose in parts of the lesson which will add an element of mystery or surprise. Learners will discover they have learned something unexpected after participating in the experience. This is important, because learners tend to lose their motivation if a teacher regularly asks them to participate in activities that have no relation to the class goal.

Principle: When you design your lesson with a goal in mind and in the initial moments of the lesson share that goal with the class in a way that makes the goal theirs, you're building motivation into your lesson structure.

Learners Learn Best
When They See Relevance

When you set an achievable goal that is important to the learner and when your lesson process involves meaningful exploration of a Bible truth in terms of the life situation of the learner, then motivation for learning is increased. As you teach, pretend that the learner is thinking, "So what does this have to do with me?" If you can answer the question, "So what?" then you've identified the relevance of the study passage.

Principle: Learners need to see a relationship between what is being learned and their personal life needs and interests.

Learners Learn Best
When They Sense Mastery

Nothing helps motivate us more than when we feel successful at something. Learners who have a sense of mastery over the content of the lesson feel motivated to learn more.

In previous chapters we've stressed the importance of using a learner-centered approach rather than a teaching-centered approach to Christian teaching. Richards said, "In a teacher-centered class, information passes one way — from teacher to learner. This doesn't give the student a chance to test their learning, to find out if they really understand the truths. But when students have a chance to participate, they can express their ideas and in this way test their learning. They prove to themselves that they understand."[1]

Principle: The learner's success in applying information to life and seeing its relevance enhances his or her sense of mastery, and motivation is increased.

Learners Learn Best
When They See Results in Their Lives

One of the most powerful motivators for learning happens when learners can see the effect in their lives of what they have studied. The power behind Jesus' teaching was that everything he taught was meant to have an immediate impact in the lives of his hearers. Jesus never taught a theory course! To help your learners be motivated, teach for results. Ask yourself, "What difference will it make in the life of my learners that they came to my class today?"

Principle: Learners must be able to see the effects that the truths learned in your class have in their lives.

Look over your lesson structure. If you can identify places in the lesson where you provide opportunities for the above to happen, then you're on your way to helping your learners be motivated for learning.

Points for Further Thought

- Do my learners seem motivated to learn? What indications are there?

- Do I state learning goals in a way that is meaningful to my learners? Give some examples.

- Is there time in the lesson for learners to discuss the relationship of the truth being taught in the lesson to their lives?

- Is there time in the lesson for learners to interact and to test their mastery of the truth studied?

- Can students see clearly how they are to respond to the truth presented?

Note

1. Lawrence O. Richards, *Creative Bible Teaching* (Chicago: Moody Press, 1970), 134–35. Used by permission of Moody Press.

Chapter 17

Epistemology:
Can You Eat a Flower?

One day when my oldest boy was about four years old, we were sitting on a park bench eating lunch. I was watching him play in the grass out of the corner of my eye while trying to feed his little brother.

At one point he picked up a dandelion, held it up to me and asked, "Daddy, can you eat a flower?"

The question intrigued me. I was stunned that it would occur to him to ask such a question. After all, everybody knows you don't eat flowers!

Or do they? In a moment of rare philosophical insight it occurred to me that he was asking an epistemological question. At four years of age he didn't carry all the assumptions "big people" have about the world. He didn't *know* that you don't eat flowers.

Remembering that there are dandelion salads and dandelion wine, I figured that there would be no harm in responding to this inquiring mind, "I don't know. What do you think?" With that, he took a bite and munched down on the flower!

Young children are natural epistemologists. Since they are not burdened by the operational assumptions we carry around with us as adults, they are continually asking questions of the highest order, those dealing with the essential matters. Those of you who have three-year-olds know what I mean. How many times in a day can a three-year-old ask "why?"

Something happens to us in the process of growing up that robs us of being good epistemologists. Experience builds up a reservoir of operational assumptions about how the world works. We cease to wonder about things like what is hot and cold and safe to handle. We cease to wonder about people's behavior and so without thinking turn around in the elevator and look at the buttons till we get to our floor, just like everyone else. We don't think deeply about what makes our car go and stop.

Very early in our lives we are sent to school and somehow learn not to ask questions. Instead, we have the questions asked of us, and, worse, we are given the answers. Eventually, most of us cease to be epistemologists and become encyclopedic collectors of factual trivia. Some trivia are more useful than others, obviously, but in the larger context of life, we seem to settle for equating learning to a cosmic game of Trivial Pursuit.

Adults have a lot to learn about learning from children. Two-year-olds are true existentialists, and four-year-olds are model epistemologists. Often, the hardest part of teaching adults is to get them to become once again childlike epistemologists.

Epistemology is the second philosophical category after metaphysics (though some, like John Locke, would argue that it should come first — and I tend to agree). It deals with matters of truth, knowing, and learning. Basically, it is concerned with learning about learning and thinking about thinking. The basic questions of epistemology are (1) Can we know? and (2) How do we know that we know? In the teaching-learning context it includes the questions, "How do we learn?" and "How do we learn how to learn?"

For the Christian teacher, this is bread and butter stuff. What does it mean to "know" something? And how do you know that your learners know? And at what point does a learner know? And how will you know when the learner knows that he or she knows? Does real knowledge consist of facts or feelings or impressions? Do we learn through intellect (using our mind), or intuition (through our feelings), or mystic processes (via our spirit and divine revelations)?

How you answer these questions is important. Your answers will give you a clue about why you teach the way you do.

In other words, answering these essential questions will reveal your operational assumptions about yourself as a teacher, your learners, and your teaching methods. How you arrive at your answers to these questions is telling: Did you do research? Did you "just know" the answers? Did you ask someone for the answer? Did the answers come to you in your dreams?

We know that there are different levels of "knowing." And we agree that it is important to strive for the higher forms of learning that lead learners to those higher levels of knowing. For example, it's one thing for a learner to memorize John 3:16. It is better if he or she were to experience the truth of that verse. But it will be better still if he or she were to apply the message and meaning of that verse in daily living.

Benjamin Bloom provided a hierarchy of learning (sometimes called a taxonomy) that helps us decide what to aim for in our teaching.[1] Going from the simplest category of learning or knowing to the highest, the hierarchy looks like this:

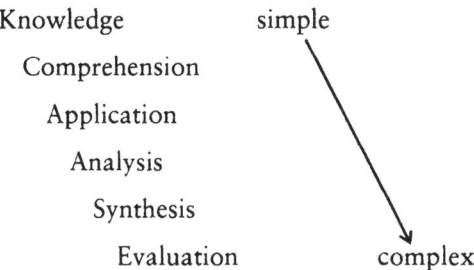

These are technical terms, and it is sometimes difficult to know what each of these levels of learning "looks" like. Appendix A (p. 165) is a helpful tool called "Cognitive Learning Actions" that can help you aim for the appropriate level of learning in your teaching. The chart lists action words appropriate to each level of learning. By choosing the level and action you can recognize at which level your learners are engaged. The chart also will provide hints as to which methods will best achieve your aim. Remember, good learning rarely happens by

Classic Epistemological Responses

	Can we know?	*How do we know?*
IDEALIST	"Yes, we can know the truth."	"We know through our intellect or mind."
REALIST	"Yes, we can know the truth to a certain extent" (scientific) or "Maybe, but we really can't know for certain or definitely" (skepticism).	"We know through our senses" (empiricism).
NEO-THOMIST	"Yes, we can know truth with certainty and definitely" (dogmatism).	"We know some truth through our senses, but the higher truth is learned through the intellect. The ultimate source of truth is revelation."
PRAGMATIST	"Yes, if by truth you mean problem solving."	"If it works, it's true. Experience is the best teacher."
EXISTENTIALIST	"Yes, but only in a personal, individual sense."	"We know the choices that we make based on our own internal, subjective awareness."

accident — you have to plan for it. Choose the level of learning you want your students to achieve. Then use an action word to write your learning outcome.

We won't solve the heady and cosmic questions of epistemology in this short chapter. But we wanted to get you thinking about it. The chart above summarizes the epistemological question as answered by some classic schools of philosophic thought. (You will easily be able to identify all of these approaches in the course of an ordinary day if you are alert to them.)

By the way, dandelions don't taste good.

Points for Further Thought

- Which school of thought most closely matches your thinking about epistemology?

- Which is least like your own thinking? Why?

- What would your teaching look like if you pushed your epistemology to its extreme logical conclusion?

- How does the way you learn reflect your epistemology?

- How is your personal epistemology evident in your teaching?

- Consider for a moment the possibility that your epistemological assumptions are wrong. How would you have to change the way you think? Learn? Teach?

Note

1. Benjamin Bloom and Associates, *Taxonomy of Educational Objectives, Handbook I: Cognitive Domain* (New York: McKay, 1956).

Chapter 18

How to Teach a Perfect Lesson Every Time

I had the opportunity to watch a master teacher at work recently. I marveled at how this teacher made the presentation look so easy and smooth and natural, like all professionals do when performing their craft. We were hooked into the lesson with the teacher's first few words. Our interest in the lesson never wavered, time stood still (at least we never noticed its passing until the class was over), and, amazingly, by the end of the lesson we learned what we were told we would.

Afterward, I reviewed the learning experience trying to determine how this teacher had managed to teach a "perfect lesson." Frankly, I couldn't come up with anything "special" or extraordinary that she did, nor anything much different from other learning experiences. There were no novel teaching methods, no dramatics, no fireworks, and no fancy electronic media were used. The lesson was entertaining, but it was not mere entertainment — we learned something. So what was this teacher's secret to teaching a "perfect lesson"?

The secret to teaching a perfect lesson is that...there is no secret! Remember the old maxim, "Genius is 10 percent inspiration and 90 percent perspiration"? Well, the same can be said for teaching: "Successful teaching is 10 percent talent (performance, technology, education, whatever) and 90 percent preparation." It's that simple, really. The best teachers are those who have put in the time preparing to teach a good lesson; it's the best way to ensure that you teach a "perfect lesson" every time. Below are some ideas for preparing your lesson.

Following these suggestions will help you teach that "perfect lesson"!

Prepare for each lesson "again for the first time." Especially if you are an experienced teacher, avoid the temptation to coast on your previously learned knowledge. What you used to know about a subject or passage of Scripture has faded somewhat (and for some of us the rate of fading gray matter is faster than for others!). "Only fresh conceptions inspire us to our best efforts."[1]

If you are growing in your spiritual life as a teacher, then what you know about a subject should be different now from the last time you taught it. You are a different person today than you were last year, more experienced, knowledgeable, and mature. To continue to teach based on what you used to know is a conscious decision to stop growing.

Don't be satisfied with what you already know. Read new sources. Try to examine Scripture passages using different study approaches. Entertain the validity of a different (even heretical) interpretation. Expand your knowledge about a familiar subject. There is always something new to learn about what we already know (or think we know).

The assumptions that we incorporate into our living, our thoughts, and our worldview can hinder us from seeing new truths and gaining new insights. Sometimes the best Christian teaching we do is when we motivate our learners to be dissatisfied with what they already know by challenging their assumptions about self, God, and their world. On occasion teach to create dissonance in your learners.

Develop a personal study plan. Set a definite time each week to do your lesson preparation. If you can establish this discipline, you'll be a more effective teacher and will lower your level of anxiety about teaching each week.

Make connections in the lesson to more familiar facts and principles through the use of analogies. In this way, you'll come up with a number of illustrations that will serve as "bridges" to application or as "windows" to insight. Identify a central truth and complete the sentence, "This is like...."

Study the lesson early in the week, and review it several times during the week until you can recount it in your own words. (Someone has said that the final product of clear thought is clear speech.) Use any and all resources available to you: books, journals, magazines, newspaper articles, other teachers, your students, your ministers, e-mail, anything and everything you have access to.

Identify the flow of the lesson. You should be able to see the natural order of the several steps in the lesson. If you can't, or it doesn't feel natural to you, then change it so it does. Go from the general to the specific, or from the specific to the general, or from the known to the unknown, or from quiet to frenzied, or from old to new — whatever is appropriate to the learning experience and learner outcomes.

Once you establish the flow of your lesson, play it out in your mind. Picture yourself with your learners in your teaching environment. See yourself teaching the lesson, guiding students in learning activities. Pay attention to how you make the transition from one step to the next. Play out the lesson in your mind in "quick time" and then in "slow motion." Based on this exercise, fine-tune the flow of your lesson.

Find the relevance of the lesson to your learners. What does what you want them to learn have to do with their daily living? Why do they need to know what you are teaching? If you can identify why they need what you are teaching, you have your motivation for the lesson: a perceived unmet need is a motivator. Answer the question, "If my students never learn this lesson, what will they lack in their lives?"

Find a way early in the lesson (certainly the first or second step) to communicate the relevance of the lesson. Better yet, design a way to help the learners identify the need for themselves that you will address in the lesson.

Choose learner participation methods to help your learners actively engage in the lesson. Your choice of methods should help carry the flow of the lesson. Use highly participatory methods at the beginning and end of your lesson — at the motivation step and the application step (see Appendix B: "Learner

Participation Methods," p. 166). Other than at these two times in the lesson, you can establish and maintain whatever teaching routine is comfortable for you and your learners. Don't feel you need to be "creative" and "entertaining" at every step of the lesson.

Aim to teach one thing at a time. Frankly, that's as much as your learners will be able to handle effectively (complete mastery of one thing is better than an ineffective acquaintance with many). When it comes to effective teaching, less is more. The human mind can handle only one new concept at a time. The maximum number of "bits of information" the mind can process at any given moment is eight (like in the "eight bits" of a computer chip). When it comes to teaching, we do well to focus on teaching one new concept at each learning session.

To help your students learn the one thing you want them to learn from each lesson, go ahead and *tell* your learners the one thing you want them to learn. Teaching is not a guessing game between teacher and learner. Let them in on the secret!

By now you've realized that, indeed, there is no magic formula for learning how to teach a "perfect lesson." Like almost anything in life, it just takes basic commitment to the task and hard work. And as with most other things, a little "know how" can go a long way. Investing in a little hard work in your preparation time will go a long way to making your classroom teaching a more effective learning experience.

Points for Further Thought

- Think about what you believed ten years ago about the following: God, Jesus Christ, your place in the world, salvation, Christian behavior. How is what you believe today different? The same?

- Examine the next lesson, workshop, or seminar you will teach. Can you identify the "one thing" you want your audience to learn?

- Assume that at the end of your next lesson a learner will ask you, "So what?" How will you respond?

Note

1. John Milton Gregory, *The Seven Laws of Teaching* (Grand Rapids: Baker Book House, 1979), 33.

Chapter 19

The Art of Asking Questions

At our weekly meeting with the senior staff psychiatrist at the mental hospital where I did my clinical pastoral training, he began — as he usually did — by asking a question. He looked our group over and asked, "What is the greatest skill every good counselor has?"

As usual, several of us would offer answers that would inevitably be wrong. One replied, "A third ear." Another said, "Empathy." Since his silence indicated that those were not the "right" answers, others in the group fired off things like: experience, compassion, unconditional positive regard, and diagnostic skills. All good answers, but they obviously were not the answers he was looking for.

According to this experienced psychiatrist, the greatest skill a good counselor has is the ability to ask appropriate questions. In the course of my tenure at the hospital, I was able to confirm that truth. Those counselors and psychologists who were perceived as being most effective had one thing in common: they were greatly skilled in the art of asking questions.

As I moved into my chosen vocational field in education, I discovered an interesting thing. Like in counseling, the greatest teachers I came across were those skilled in the art of asking questions. I remember in particular one third-grade teacher at the school where I was a principal. She was a master in the art of asking questions. Her technique was excellent. She would lead her students through any subject matter by skillfully asking questions that led them from simple responses to deeper and more analytical discussion. The lesson developed so smoothly and subtly that the students were unaware that their level of participation moved from simple to higher order learning in a matter of a few minutes.

The craft of Christian teaching challenges us to engage our students in discussion and dialogue. In the teaching-learning process, dialogue is where the most meaningful learning takes place in matters of a person's relationship to God, self, and others. And so, the effective Christian teacher's greatest skill is the ability to ask good questions that enable dialogue. Unfortunately, asking good questions also is one of the most difficult skills to acquire.

As teachers, most of us tend to get in the habit of asking "closed" questions early in our teaching. Closed questions are those that elicit "closed responses," that is, responses that can be answered in one word or with a simple phrase. We do this to children when we ask "How was school today?" (response: "Fine"), or "Did you have fun?" ("Yes," or "Uh huh"). Closed questions are satisfied by a minimal response ... *any* minimal response. When we get in the habit of asking closed questions we in effect control our learners' responses and limit critical and reflective thinking. This kind of questioning is useful when cross-examining a hostile witness on the stand when you want to control information, but it spells death to dialogue.

How you ask a question is important. Our minds process questions in distinct ways. For example, asking a question twice only serves to confuse the hearer and keeps him or her from processing the question efficiently. If you change or rephrase the question you asked before allowing the learner to answer, you in effect change the question and have asked two different questions. The learner is left wondering which question to answer and which to discount.

If you listen to yourself teach, you'll probably be surprised at how often you repeat a question or rephrase it before allowing a learner to respond. Learning to ask one question at a time is one of the most difficult skills for a teacher to master, but it is the most basic technique for asking questions effectively.

The most efficient questioning technique is when the teacher asks a question once, waits for a response or an answer from the learner, and then responds specifically (gives feedback) to the answer before posing another question. Not giving feedback to a learner's response to your question does not cue the learner as to how his or her answer is received: was it right? Was it wrong? Was it incomplete?

Here are contrasting good and poor examples of a question-and-answer interchange between teacher (T) and learner (L):

Poor	Good
T: "What is the Southern Kingdom called? Who remembers from last week?"	T: "What is the name of the Southern Kingdom?"
L (after deciding which question to answer): "Judah."	L: "Judah."
T (ignores right answer, no feedback): "And what is the name of the Northern Kingdom?"	T: "That's correct! (gives feedback). I can tell you were paying attention last week. And now who can tell me the name of the Northern Kingdom?"

These are simple examples, but they help illustrate the process of good questioning skills. Asking questions effectively becomes critical when the concepts you are trying to teach are complex and abstract, like justice, mercy, love, sacrifice, stewardship, good, evil, salvation, and justification.

In your teaching, the depth of dialogue will be determined by the quality of the questions you ask. Effective teachers choose those methods and questions that facilitate discussion. There are at least six categories of questions you can choose from, each corresponding to one of the levels of learning (see the chart on the next page). One way of learning the art of asking questions is to do what my third-grade teacher did: intentionally choose to move your learners through the dialogue by asking questions from each category, moving to higher order learning questions as you go. In your questions, move from the simple to the complex as the discussion moves along.

With reference to the story of the Prodigal Son, here are examples of questions from each category. Notice how the

Categories of Questions: From Simple to Complex

INFORMATION	Ask learners to list data and facts specific to the content
COMPREHENSION	Ask learners about the meanings of the content
APPLICATION	Ask learners for places and domains where the content is relevant
ANALYSIS	Ask learners to distinguish meaning in the content
SYNTHESIS	Ask learners to make connections about the content
EVALUATION	Ask learners to make judgments about the content

questions move the learner from lower to higher order engagement in the story:

- *Information level:* Who were the three people involved in this story?

- *Comprehension level:* Was it significant that the main character of the story was the youngest son?

- *Application level:* What opportunities do you have to forgive someone who repents a wrong done to you?

- *Analysis level:* What was the main point Jesus wanted to make with this story? What relationship question was answered in this story?

- *Synthesis level:* Can you think of ways this parable relates to other teachings in the Bible about how God treats us? About how we should treat others?

- *Evaluation level:* What is your opinion about Jesus' use of this story? What is your opinion about the point Jesus was trying to make?

When will you know that you've arrived at a good discussion level? One good sign is when the students themselves start asking questions. At this point an effective teacher will engage another fine skill in the art of asking questions: answering a question with a question that will help your learners arrive at the answer for themselves (a Socratic method of teaching).

As you develop your skills in the art of asking questions, you will want to keep the following in mind:

- Write out key basic questions as part of your lesson planning. Improvise or expand on these while teaching.

- Use simple closed questions at the beginning of your class to get everyone to give a response and participate in the lesson. The longer a learner takes to participate the less likely he or she ever will.

- Ask one question at a time.

- After you ask a question, close your mouth, look at your learners, and wait for a response.

- Don't answer your own question just because there is silence. Wait. Someone will respond.

- Don't be afraid to ask "dumb" questions (or shocking questions) to start a discussion.

Points for Further Thought

- Examine the teaching resource you use. Identify the levels of the questions they lead you to ask.

- In terms of the Christian life, which level of questioning do you feel is most effective to prompt growth? Why?

- Reflect on your style of asking questions. Are you able to ask one question at a time and wait for a response?

Chapter 20

Maximizing Learner Retention

No, this chapter isn't about one of those anxiety-causing health concerns like water weight gain. Retention in the teaching-learning process refers to the "amount" of information or knowledge retained by a learner after a learning experience.

Retention can be measured by the percentage of accuracy in the recall of information by the learner over a given period of time. For example, after a lesson or content-oriented learning experience, the teacher administers a test or quiz. If the student can recall the content (knowledge, information) learned and score a 90 percent on the test, then we would say that the student has a high retention rate. If, however, the student were tested again a week later on the same material, but achieved only a 30 percent score on the test, then we would have to adjust our thinking and say that the actual retention rate is low.

Knowing about retention rates helps us understand that some forms of learning are more effective than others in helping students retain knowledge. In the end, most of us would not be satisfied with our learners just knowing something for the moment. We want our teaching to make lasting impressions in the lives of our learners. In Christian teaching, we offer truths that are for life and living, so it is important that learners be able to remember the teachings and truths we try to impart.

How we teach a truth or principle is just as important as the truth itself. What good will the truth do for you if you will not remember it because of the way it is taught? How effective is the teacher who knows the truth, but cannot impart it in such a way that the learner will always remember it? Knowing how to teach the truths of the faith is just as important — perhaps more important — than knowing them for yourself. If only you know them, what difference will that make in the lives of those around you? None!

This is especially relevant when we realize the distinctions in the learning processes of children and adults. We all marvel at the facility with which most children seem to learn and are frustrated as adults to discover that some things seem harder to learn as we get older (try challenging an eight-year-old to a play-off on a new video game and see who learns the game faster). But the fact is that there is no evidence (aside from organic brain disorders) that learning or learning ability declines as a person moves into adulthood and continues to age.

In fact, adults tend to be *better* learners because of their wealth of experience which allows them to use the most basic dynamic of learning: building on what they already know (called "crystallized intelligence"). Adults also have a more sophisticated repertoire of learning modalities from which to choose when learning. It may appear that adults are slower at learning new things, and that may be true in a sense. But this in part is due to the fact that adults process new ideas and facts in a more complex way than do children and that adults choose what they will learn (and not learn) more than children are able.

We know that a learner retains about 10 percent of what he or she hears, 20 percent of what he or she reads, and 50 percent of what he or she sees. But even a 50 percent retention is too low when we are teaching things of significance. Luckily, we know that higher learner retention is possible than what hearing, reading, and seeing can achieve: a learner will retain 90 percent of what he or she does. Active learning and participation are the keys to higher retention of learning.

The matter becomes more dramatic when we look at the rate of retention. Time, combined with weak learning strategies, has a detrimental effect on retention rates. The chart on the next page illustrates the retention rates of various learning approaches over a period of three hours as compared to a period of after three days. When a student only hears (listens), the retention rate drops from 70 percent after three hours to

Retention Rates

	After 3 hours	After 3 days
Hearing Only	70%	10%
Seeing Only	72%	20%
Hearing and Seeing	85%	65%
Doing and Participation	95%	90%

10 percent on the third day. Even combining hearing and seeing (observing) will help the student retain only a little over half (65 percent). But when the student participates in the learning experience, the retention rate after three days remains at 90 percent.

What we need to remember as teachers is that the more the learner participates actively in the learning experience, the higher the retention rate will be over an extended period of time. In other words, learners learn best when actively engaged in learning for themselves. Our most effective teaching happens when we provide opportunities for learners to discover the truths of the Christian life for themselves.

In order to increase your learners' retention of learning, you may have to adjust your teaching from the role of the "Grand Imparter of Knowledge and Learning" to that of guide or facilitator. Below are some guidelines to help you plan learning experiences that will help your students remember the lesson.

- *Change your teaching style:* Emphasize learning over teaching. Take the focus off teacher performance and concentrate on creating opportunities for learning.

- *Emphasize process over content:* Use learning approaches that guide the students to discover the truth for themselves. Show, don't tell. Move learners from experience to reflection to insight.

- *Talk less to teach more:* Give your students more opportunities for dialogue, questions, and sharing. Ask more questions and give fewer answers.

- *Use triads and dyads:* To let everyone get in on the act, break up your class into smaller groups. Four persons is an ideal number for a small group, but you can use groups of two and three effectively.

- *Always debrief:* When using small groups, always debrief the class by asking each group to share the results of its work. Ask clarifying questions during debriefing. Challenge the group to reach a consensus based on the input from the small groups.

- *Less is more:* Strive to teach one thing at a time and do it to death! A lesson on "life, the universe, and everything" will result in your pupils learning less of anything about everything.

- *Build on the basics:* Repetition and memorization are your most basic tools for learning and teaching. Don't neglect them or discount their importance; rather, build on their foundation. Use mnemonic devices to jump-start the acquisition of content and to help your learners move quickly to higher levels of learning.

Points for Further Thought

- In what ways do you learn differently now than when you were a child?

- What methods have you used to help your learners effectively memorize important information?

- How valuable do you think memorization is? Why?

- Can you recite something you learned before you were six years old? Before you were five years old? Earlier?

- In your teaching, do you tend to fill up the class time by talking, or do you tend to find ways to help your learners discover truths for themselves?

Chapter 21

Adding Movement and Style to Your Teaching

Have you ever been "taken for a ride"? You know what I mean — led by the nose; swallowed something hook, line, and sinker.

I still remember with chagrin my first encounter with a salesman in my first management job. He took one look at me and those little dollar signs appeared in his eyes. He had style, and his sales pitch moved flawlessly from one step to the next: smile, hearty handshake, small talk, corny joke, relational question ("How're the wife and kids?"), sales pitch. And then he popped the question: "How many do you want to buy today?" He pulled out the order sheet, all filled out just waiting for my signature. I didn't have a chance. I ordered a case of stuff I didn't need — but I learned a good lesson in the deal.

A great communicator once said that how you communicate is just as important as what you say. In terms of teaching that may mean that how you teach is as important as the content of your lesson. It's easy to see how that can be true in Christian teaching. To teach about God's love lovingly is more effective than presenting that same message with an attitude of intolerance and impatience. In the Christian faith, "the medium is the message."

The style you choose to carry the content of your lesson can either hinder or help bring the message home in the life of your learners. My salesman friend knew how to bring the message home by moving me from suspicion and discomfort to acceptance and action. Giving attention to style and movement in the teaching process can help you become a more effective teacher.

Style refers to the way you choose to engage in the process of teaching. Each style has its own movement. *Movement* refers to those components that help the lesson "flow" during the learning experience, how one part of the lesson leads into the next and how all parts together lead the learners to where you want them to go. For example, you can choose to use a movement in a lesson that will start out as slow or subdued and flow eventually to fast-paced or highly interactive. The movement you choose should help you carry the message of your content.

Below eight styles of teaching are discussed.[1] Each has its own movement. Within each movement, choose the learning methods that best fit what you want to accomplish in that part of the lesson (see Appendix B: "Learner Participation Methods," p. 166). Each style can be used for a single lesson or for a series of lessons. Choose the style that can best help your learners assimilate the message you want to teach.

Linking

Try to link the lesson topic to the life experience of your learners. The lesson begins with a focus on the learner's experience and ends with calling for a response to the content. The movements within this style are:

1. *Entry:* Ask introductory questions or provide activities that will help the learners share their experiences on the matter at hand: "What is your experience with...?" "What did you do when...?" "How did you handle that situation?" "How did you feel...?"

2. *Exploration:* Use those methods that will lead learners to study the theme — research report, lecture, video clips. Then lead a discussion to introduce and explore the content.

3. *Diving in:* Go deeper into the content by leading your learner to engage in the content. Use interactive participatory methods: making a sculpture, picture, or collage, engaging in a pro-con discussion, forming a panel of speakers, or giving a report.

4. *Application:* Help the learners explore their responses to the content from a Christian perspective. Call for a personal response to the message of the lesson.

Shared Life Experience

The shared life experience style is similar to linking, but the movement and focus is on the shared group experience. The emphasis is on the experience of the community rather than that of the individual. The movement within this style may look like this:

1. *Exploring shared experiences:* Ask learners to share their experiences. Discuss how they are similar and how they are different.

2. *Theological reflection:* Allow the learners to explore their experiences and feelings surrounding what they have shared. Move them to reflect how their experiences informed their faith, or how their faith informed their experiences.

3. *Storymaking:* Guide your learners to make a connection between the shared experiences of the group and the biblical story. Ask open-ended questions to help them make the connections.

4. *Application:* Allow the group to voice applications of what they learned in making connections between their story and the biblical story. Challenge the group to reach a consensus regarding the relationship between their stories and the biblical story.

Study Contracting

Study contracting works best with a small group (between twelve and fifteen) and more mature learners. This format is ideal for short-term studies. The movement within this style may look like this:

1. *Formation:* Lead the group to clarify expectations for learning and for the format of the learning experience: time, place, number of meetings, level of commitment, methods used, leadership, attendance, etc.

2. *Engagement:* The learners enter the learning process in accordance with the contract they agreed to. If the group gets stuck in procedural matters, help members renegotiate the initial agreement if necessary.

3. *Evaluation:* When the learning cycle is completed, provide a way for the group to evaluate the learning experience. Share thoughts and feelings about what worked and what didn't. Lead the group members to share what they have learned through this experience in terms of content, new understanding, or insights.

4. *Closure:* Guide the group to decide whether to continue under a new contract or to disband as a learning group.

Problem Solving

Problem solving calls for a high level of commitment and participation from learners. It appeals to certain kinds of learners, but can provide a good challenge for most. The movement within this style may look like this:

1. *Presentation of the problem:* Lead the group to select a problem that arises out of discussion or propose a problem for the group based on a current situation.

2. *Analysis:* Provide ways for the group to analyze as many dimensions of the problem as you can. As a rule, eight people can come up with an almost exhaustive list of the various aspects of any problem.

3. *Information gathering and research:* Either as a group or through individual assignments, explore the problem as addressed in Scripture, books, articles, films, literature, history, etc. Provide a forum for sharing and reporting the research.

4. *Conclusions:* Lead the group to evaluate the research and then guide the group in formulating a statement based on their

conclusions. The statement can be a recommendation or a list of possible solutions to the problem; you could also prepare a restatement of the assumptions and perceptions about what the problem is.

5. *Application:* Prompt the group to make a list of possible applications to life situations based on their conclusions.

Inquiry and Application

The inquiry and application style is similar to the shared life experience and problem solving approaches, but it takes things deeper in that the learners are called upon to apply their findings in a real-life situation. The movement within this style may look like this:

1. *Theme negotiation:* Lead the learners as a group to reach a consensus on the theme of the inquiry.

2. *Shared experience:* Allow the group to share their experiences relating to the theme.

3. *Investigation:* Have the group investigate as much as they can about the theme through research and study. They identify the critical elements of the theme.

4. *Verification:* Provide ways for the group to test their findings and conclusions against research from other sources on the same theme.

5. *Application:* Help the group finds ways to apply the findings of their research to a real-life situation they share in common.

Concepts Development

The concepts development style can help equip learners for theological reflection. Most matters of faith, belief, doctrine, and theology require the ability to deal with abstract concepts. The movement within this style may look like this:

1. *Collecting insights:* Invite your learners to share their understanding, experiences, and stories with regard to the concept you want them to learn.

2. *Concept study:* Provide a variety of resources (texts, dictionaries, readings, video) for your learners to research the various meanings and uses of the concept. Have learners list the characteristics of the concept based on their findings.

3. *Concept development:* Guide the learners to use the data gained from the previous step to define the concept in their own words. Have them test their definition based on their research findings. Challenge them to strive for accuracy.

4. *Reflection:* Lead the learners to examine the process of how they reached their definition. Guide them in a discussion about how this process might help them approach other faith questions.

Field Trip Experience

The field trip teaching style takes the learning experience outside of the classroom. The movement within this style may look like this:

1. *Briefing:* Lead the group to discuss the anticipated field experience, clarifying the purpose and procedures for the excursion.

2. *Field trip experience:* Visit the site of the field experience. Depending on the desired learning outcome, this can be another church's worship service, a community soup kitchen, a homeless shelter, a nursing home, a museum, etc.

3. *Debriefing:* Prompt the group to share observations and insights from their field trip experience; explore knowledge gained, new understanding, and feelings. Prompt the group to formulate new questions based on their observations.

4. *Theological reflection:* Lead the group in discussing the implications of their observations for their Christian lives. Use higher order questions of meaning, understanding, and application.

Peer Groups Teaching

The peer groups teaching style takes advantage of the personal resources the learners bring to the group and challenges each member to become a teacher. The movement within this style may look like this:

1. *Indicators:* Introduce the focus of the theme, the concept, or the problem at hand to the group.

2. *Teams formation:* Form small peer groups and assign them to research the theme or problem. Teams can negotiate among themselves which parts of the research assignments they will take.

3. *Reporting:* Facilitate a forum in which each peer group shares insights with other groups. Include an opportunity for a question-and-answer period.

4. *Application:* Form the peer groups again to reconsider and extend their understanding based on the forum presentation and on the reported information. Have them make applications to the Christian life.

5. *Synthesis debriefing:* Assemble the entire group. Lead them to formulate key ideas from the groups and the forum. Have them consider and weigh the applications for Christian living.

The most valuable aspect of using these teaching-learning styles with their movements is that they enable the teacher to move the focus away from teaching toward learning. All of these styles allow the teacher to become a facilitator of the learning experience. The learners take responsibility for their own learning, as well as the learning of those with whom they work. Authentic Christian teaching allows the learner freedom to learn from self, others, and the Spirit. As you consider your approach to teaching, avail yourself of how these styles use movement to carry the learner along in the process of learning.

Points for Further Thought

- Name some benefits of using these styles of teaching with your learners.

- Can you anticipate any disadvantages to using any of these styles of teaching? Explain.

- If you have never used these styles of teaching, how would your teaching change if you were to attempt them?

- Do you think giving more responsibility for learning to your students will work? Why or why not?

- These styles of learning may be challenging to some learners. What are some characteristics of learners for whom these styles would be a difficult learning experience?

Note

1. Adapted from Kevin Treston, *A New Vision of Religious Education: Theory, History, Practice, and Spirituality for DREs, Catechists, and Teachers* (Mystic, Conn.: Twenty-Third Publications, 1993).

Chapter 22

Creating Focal Points
for Teaching

I enjoy watching a good magician performing his or her craft. Interestingly, it's not the big productions like making the Statue of Liberty disappear or transforming an assistant into a tiger that really intrigue me. Rather, it's the close-up, in-your-face, sleight-of-hand tricks that get me every time. Those tricks require focus and attention. But of course no matter how closely I think I'm watching, I always miss the trick.

Teaching is like that in a way. Except that unlike magicians who use their skill to force us to focus away from the truth, good teachers try to help their learners to focus on and see the truth being taught. And just like magicians, the teachers can use focal points in the teaching process to accomplish this.

Focal points are those things you do or provide throughout the lesson to help your learners stay on task and focused on the matter at hand. They take many forms and, depending on what you are trying to teach, can be used to help the learner focus on content or on the physical or the emotional dimensions of the learning experience.

Focal points have the following characteristics:

- They are used throughout the lesson.

- They relate to the truth you are trying to teach.

- They are overt in their meaning (use them to "whack your student over the head" with the truth).

- They can be simple.

- They make a physical or emotional connection for the learner.

- They can be easily remembered and recalled.

Content Focal Points

Use content focal points to help your learners key in on the central message of your lesson. You can use a poster or a handout with the central concept, the key verse, or the underlying principle you are trying to teach. Remember, this is not subtle. If you're teaching a principle, then write it out; don't make your learners have to guess.

If your focal point is a poster, point or refer to it throughout the lesson. If you use a handout with the central verse on it, stop at appropriate points in your lesson and have the class read it out loud. Content focal points can help your learners memorize important facts or information. But best of all, they will help reinforce understanding.

Once when I taught an adult church history course, I used a simple expanding timeline as a content focal point. At the start of every lesson I would write a list of dates on the blackboard. I would read the dates and the learners would respond by reciting the associated significant historical event. In the middle of a lesson, if I referred to a particular event, I would point to its corresponding date on the expanding timeline. As the course progressed, the list of dates got longer and the learners memorized more facts. In this way, they were able to get a sense of perspective of historical events and movements. This, in turn, improved their understanding of historical progression and movements.

Physical Focal Points

A central wall can provide a physical focal point for your teaching-learning experience. On it you can hang a unit poster, a content focal point like a scrambled Bible verse, or a painting or print that will serve as your focal point during the lesson.

An effective physical focal point can sit at the center of the room on a short table. It can be a lump of clay that takes shape during the lesson, an art object, a display, a collection of objects that relate to the lesson, or a sealed box or envelope around which you will build the lesson.

You can use the physical focal point to lead learners to ask questions and make observations. For example, suppose you place a child's toy elephant and toy giraffe on a table as your focal points. You can divide the class into two teams — one for the elephant, one for the giraffe — and have them come up with as many statements as they can to answer the question, "How is an elephant or giraffe like a Christian?" As the lesson progresses, refer back to your learners' observations about how an elephant or giraffe is like a Christian.

Physical focal points are important because they provide visual and kinesthetic (touching) dimensions to your teaching. This instantly expands the repertoire of learning options from which your students can choose. In the same church history course mentioned above, I used oddly shaped pieces of colored construction paper to create a large floor map. I wrote the names of the countries under discussion and had the learners construct a map on the floor in the center of the room. The map didn't have to be accurate, but it provided a physical focal point I referred to during the lesson. This gave the learners a visual reference point during class discussions.

Regardless of what you use as a physical focal point, reveal as soon as you can its connection with the truth or point of the lesson and refer to it often.

Emotional Focal Points

You can use emotional focal points to help your learners move into a deeper level of learning. Remember that the spirit of a person resides more in the realm of the emotional than in the cerebral. Emotional focal points elicit an emotional response on the part of the learner, so they are not always comfortable.

An emotional focal point can be a personal illustration, an interactive activity, or an experience (listening to music, engaging in a role play) that will illicit an emotional response from your learners during the class period. An emotional focal point can be a reference to a shared experience that will recall an emotional memory.

Remember that focal points are not subtle strategies. If you are going to use an emotional focal point to help your learners, tell them you are doing so. Then, refer back to the emotional focal point often during the lesson. "How did you feel when ... ?" Or, "Remember how you felt when ... ?"

Using focal points in your teaching will help your learners maintain interest in the truth you are trying to teach through your lesson. Focal points have the added benefit of instantly expanding the learning styles repertoire from which your learners can choose. In addition, they will help you, the teacher, to follow through on one of the most effective teaching strategies: teach *one* thing at a time.

Points for Further Thought

Think about your next teaching opportunity:

- What content focal point can you use to help your learners remain focused on the aim of the lesson?

- What can you use as a physical focal point for the lesson?

- What can you use as an emotional focal point?

- Write in one sentence of seven words or less the one thing you want your learners to learn.

Chapter 23

How to Teach Values: A Seven-Step Process

At a meeting of parents and educators, I heard again the litany of laments about "today's kids" — how they can't read, don't know right from wrong, have no discipline, show no courtesy, lack reasoning skills, don't know what they believe, are cynical, don't take advice, etc. You've heard them all before. If you're a parent or teacher, you may have uttered some of these yourself.

Some parents blamed the schools, some educators blamed parents, everybody blamed society. Who's really to blame? Personally, I'm not sure who's to blame — maybe all of them. But I'm certain that blaming is not the answer.

As I observe adults and teenagers whom I admire there is one characteristic that stands above all others in making me feel comfortable being around them: they all have a grasp of their personal values. They can articulate the values they live by. In conversation, they can reason through questions and issues working from their core values of what is right and wrong, good and bad, or good enough and better.

It is unsettling to think that children in our society may have a harder time developing their sense of values than those of previous generations. Our children are exposed to more information, images, symbols, and phenomena than could even be imagined a generation ago. And many are exposed to all these without the benefit of guiding interpretations from significant persons in their lives as to "what it all means." Today's children have more choices and alternatives than their parents had at their age. This makes them less provincial and more sophisticated in some ways. But in another sense, the constant and complex array of choices makes the act of choosing (discerning) more difficult. We are in danger of creating a generation stuck in an adolescent stage of thinking and believing — one that holds that to know about something is to comprehend it, or that to be familiar with a truth is to have practiced it. How can a child be expected to know what to believe in a world where fantasy is valued more than reality?

It's not hard to spot the person who has not developed a personal value system. Raths, Harmin, and Simon, in their book *Values and Teaching*, identified eight characteristic patterns of persons who have not developed a set of core values:

1. *Apathetic:* These people are characterized by listlessness and seem uninterested in the world around them. They are willing to drift through life, letting the world carry them along with apparent little interest in where they will wind up.

2. *Flighty:* While these people may seem interested in many things, their interest lasts for brief periods of time. They can get involved in something with great enthusiasm, but can quickly become uninterested and unmotivated as they abandon it for the latest fad or another "new favorite thing."

3. *Uncertain:* These are the people who seem unable to make up their minds when confronted with choices. Lacking direction or focus, they are unable to choose even from among several good options.

4. *Inconsistent:* These persons are uncritically involved in many things that are mutually inconsistent. Some of the things they participate in may even be mutually destructive. Patterns in their lives tend to be incompatible: they say they believe one thing but act out another; or they behave one way one week and a contradictory way the next.

5. *Drifters:* These persons show a pattern of behavior characterized by unenthusiastic drifting from one thing to another. They tend to lack an ability to plan and to commit to persons, causes, or communities.

6. *Overconformers:* Without a clear idea of what they want

to do in life, these persons join themselves to whichever happens to be the prevailing viewpoint. They are easily swayed to conform to the most attractive group of the moment.

7. *Overdissenters:* These are chronic naggers and irrational dissenters. They tend to find their identity and purpose in reacting to the ideas and beliefs of others. They consistently define themselves on the basis of others rather than on the basis of self.

8. *Role players:* These are persons who cover their lack of a sense of self and the resultant lack of clarity about life goals by assuming artificial roles. They assume roles by taking their cue from others about who they are: class clown, stoic, nerd, bully, jock, or brain.[1]

The dictionary defines values as "the social principles, goals, or standards held or accepted by an individual, class, society, etc."[2] A value includes a person's understanding of right and wrong, beauty, ultimate reality, and what is of worth. Persons with a strong sense of personal values act consistently out of those core values.

Values do not come as standard equipment with persons. They are developed out of personal life choices in children and adults alike. These choices, in order to develop into a value, must involve alternatives or options that are prized by the person choosing, have clearly understood consequences, and are genuinely and freely available for choosing.

How Values Are Formed

As Christian teachers, it is important that we understand how a value is formed. Knowing how values are formed will enable us to figure out ways to teach our learners to enable them to choose Christian values for living. According to Raths, Harmin, and Simon, the process of valuing develops in the three-step framework of (1) choosing, (2) prizing, and (3) acting. Within this framework, seven components must be present for a value to exist.

Choosing

1. *Choosing freely.* Values must be freely chosen; they cannot be coerced. Learners must have the opportunity to make a choice freely.

2. *Choosing from among alternatives.* Values result only when choices exist; bona fide alternatives must exist from which to choose. Learners must be exposed to legitimate alternatives from which to choose.

3. *Choosing after thoughtful consideration of the consequences of each alternative.* Values do not develop through intuition or guessing; they are formed only after weighing the range of alternatives and their consequences. Learners need to be guided through the hard work of thinking through choices and their consequences.

Prizing

4. *Prizing and cherishing.* A value is a positive part of the person. Values feel good; they make us feel happy to own them. They are cherished because they guide our lives. Learners need to feel positive about the values they choose.

Acting

5. *Affirming.* Values that are freely chosen and with which we are pleased are affirmed: we are willing to publicly share our values. Learners need opportunities to express and publish their values.

6. *Acting upon choices.* When we have formed a value, we "put our money where our mouth is" and we "walk the talk," that is, we give evidence in our living of what we truly value. Ideas, truths, and learning that do not manifest themselves in the way we live are not values. Learners need ways to examine their lives to determine which values are real for them.

7. *Repeating.* Values become patterned in our lives. They become part of our life structure and manifest themselves in several areas of our lives: public and private, recreational and vocational. Learners need opportunities to practice their values in all areas of their lives.

Teaching for Values

It can be argued that Christian teaching is, in large measure, the nurturing of believers in a Christ-centered value system. The most important things we teach persons are not facts about the faith, but those beliefs and values that will help them live out their lives in conformity to the spirit of Christ. The power of Christian teaching lies in helping persons discover the center in their lives that will help them make better and higher choices for and about God, others, and self.

In teaching values, the teacher must work out of an informed understanding of how values are formed. Based on the seven-step process mentioned above, the teacher must guide the learner — whether child, youth, or adult — in a process that leads to a value-making experience. Below is a sample seven-step process for teaching a value during any teaching-learning experience:

1. Encourage the learners to make choices, and to make them freely.

2. Help the learners discover and examine available alternatives when faced with choices.

3. Help the learners weigh alternatives thoughtfully, reflecting on the consequences of each.

4. Encourage the learners to consider what it is that they prize and cherish.

5. Give the learners the opportunities to make public affirmations of their choices.

6. Encourage the learners to act, behave, and live in accordance with their choices.

7. Help the learners critically examine repeated behaviors or patterns in their lives.

Methodology for Teaching

While it is true that values are attained primarily in living life's experiences, teachers can use certain methods to help the learner attain a value. One of the most effective methods for guiding the learner through this seven-step process is the "clarifying response." In this method, the teacher makes open-ended questions that prompt the student to make clarifying responses. In using this method, the teacher avoids "preaching," criticizing, defending his or her own values, or judging the learner's values. The responsibility is put on the learner to examine his or her behavior or beliefs and to decide what he or she wants. Some of the gospel accounts of Jesus' encounters with people provide good examples of this approach (John 3:1–15; 4:1–26; 5:2–9; 7:53–8:11; 9:1–34; 20:24–29).

As with any method, using clarifying responses effectively takes practice. Here, from Raths, Harmin, and Simon, are some examples of clarifying responses:

- "Is that something you prize?"

- "Are you glad about that?"

- "How did you feel when that happened?"

- "Did you consider any alternatives?"

- "Have you felt this way for a long time?"

- "Was that something that you yourself selected or chose?"

- "Did you have to choose that; was it a free choice?"

- "Do you do anything about that idea?"

- "Can you give me some examples of that idea?"

- "What do you mean by _____ ; define that word?"[3]

Helping your learners formulate and discover a value can be a life-changing experience. Part of the challenge will be for you to be clear about your own values before you can help others with theirs.

Points for Further Thought

- List the guiding values in your life.

- Recall how you spent your time during the past week. If values manifest themselves in living, then what values are evidenced in your living?

- Look ahead to your next teaching opportunity. Will it help your learners develop Christian values? If not, what can you change to allow your learners the chance to form values?

- Are you more comfortable telling your learners what they should value or in allowing them to discover their values for themselves?

- Examine the passages in the Gospel of John cited in this chapter (p. 133). Do you think Jesus more often told people what to believe or do you think he let them make up their own minds?

Notes

1. L. Raths, M. Harmin, and S. Simon, *Values and Teaching: Working with Values in the Classroom* (Columbus, Ohio: Charles E. Merrill, 1966).

2. *Webster's New World Dictionary*, second college edition (Cleveland: William Collins, 1979).

3. Raths, Harmin, and Simon, *Values and Teaching*, 56–62.

Part 5

Methods

Chapter 24

Effective Learning
through Small Groups

Authentic Christian instruction acknowledges the distinctiveness of teaching for faith. The teaching methods most effective for spiritual development are relational ones: those that are experiential, personal, and interactive. In addition, authentic Christian teaching takes place in the context of a faith community. One of the great truths about spiritual growth is that we can't go it alone. The *I-Ching* says, "The superior man joins with his friends for discussion and practice.... Knowledge should be a refreshing and vitalizing force. It becomes so only ... with congenial friends with whom one holds discussion and practices application of the truths of life. In this way learning becomes many-sided and takes on a cheerful lightness, whereas there is always something ponderous and one-sided about the learning of the self-taught."[1] Using small groups consistently in Christian teaching will allow learners to better avail themselves of what their faith community has to offer. Authentic Christian teaching needs to provide and use small groups as a primary methodology.

Learning occurs when a change has taken place in the learner. Change brings about new insights, new ideas, new goals, and new behavior. "Learning takes place when the following changes occur: (1) addition of information, (2) increase in understandings, (3) acceptance of new attitudes, (4) acquisition of new appreciations, and (5) doing something with what has been learned."[2]

According to Martha Leypoldt in *40 Ways to Teach in Groups*, "The teacher-learning process is a cooperative effort in which not only the leader but also the group members must be involved as active participants if learning is to take place. Both the leader and the group members are learners, but the leader with additional knowledge and experience plays a different role as a learner."[3]

One of Jesus' favorite teaching methods was the story. He recognized the power of story to impact the deepest levels within persons. Sharing spiritual life stories seems to take place best in small groups (fifteen or less) where there is a process of intimate interaction among learners. This process becomes the method of the group learning dynamic. The committed use of small groups for learning holds the greatest potential for revitalizing Christian teaching in the church and other Christian learning communities.

Any content information you need to give your learners can efficiently be taught in a small group. After this, the most important dimension of the small group method — engaging learners in the relational learning process — can be used to great advantage. The goal of the small group must be consistent with the goal of Christian teaching: to help the learner hear and respond to God and others in the context of relationship.

A change in teaching style can often mean the difference between students learning or not learning. A number of learning processes that are possible only in small groups can foster the kind of learning that brings about change (learning = change, remember?). Here are some distinct benefits of using small groups in your teaching:

1. Small groups provide the intimate and supportive environment in which learners can feel free to share meaningfully their spiritual life stories.

2. Small groups provide one of the most efficient ways for communicating information and processing ideas. Communication relationships grow exponentially with each person in the group. A group of four persons has twelve communication links in its group, while a group of five

has twenty communication relationships to deal with. A teacher trying to communicate in a class of fifteen learners has 210 relationships to contend with!

3. In a small group, learners have the opportunity to discover their own reactions to the material that is presented and are encouraged to reflect on its significance for what is happening in their own lives.

4. Small groups become the mediating and interpreting community for the personal religious experiences of the individual group member. Group members expand the pool of experience and knowledge available to each individual.

5. As the immediate expression of the learner's faith community, the small group can help negotiate the imagery for the learner's individual worldview and life metaphor.

Instructional small groups are those groups you create from within the larger class for specific learning activities. Depending on the size of the class, these groups can consist of anywhere from three to fifteen members. Instructional groups are part of the overall learning experience in the lesson, so their work must flow smoothly as part of the lesson. You can use small instructional groups to:

- call learners to respond to lesson content

- have learners share personal life examples

- help learners make personal life application of the lesson content

- process discussion more efficiently

- help learners think about an issue to reach consensus

- challenge learners to solve a problem or suggest solutions

Guidelines for Working with Instructional Small Groups

1. State the group goal clearly (unless discovery or creative dissonance is part of the learning experience). Try to limit the assignment to a single goal or at most two. Be specific about what you are asking the group to do.

2. Outline the process for the small group assignment. Sometimes you will want to give specific steps for the group to follow.

3. Provide the groups with resources. Give each group everything they'll need to complete their assignment, including writing instruments and research materials or handouts.

4. Give a time limit. Give groups a sufficient amount of time to complete assignments, but don't give them too much time. If you find that most groups have finished the assignment, go ahead and call time to maintain the class momentum and avoid down time.

5. Monitor the groups. When working with small groups within a larger group setting, walk around and eavesdrop on the group conversation. This will help the groups stay on task and makes you available to clarify procedure or content questions. Monitoring the groups by walking around will make you available to help "sick" groups — those that cannot seem to get on with the task at hand for a variety of reasons: a monopolizing member, an unfortunate grouping of introverts, or a sidetracked group.

6. Debrief and evaluate. Always debrief your small groups. This affirms the value of the work they've done and carries the small group learning experience into the larger class grouping. Use a flip chart to record answers from each group. Ask clarifying and summarizing questions.

Using small groups as a consistent teaching strategy will help change the focus from teaching to learning. The natural small group dynamics that take place among learners are consistent with authentic Christian instruction. Effective Christian teachers will avail themselves of the power of small groups to facilitate meaningful learning.

Notes

1. Richard Wilhelm, *The I-Ching, or Book of Changes*, trans. Cary F. Baynes, Bollingen Series 19, 3d ed. (Princeton, N.J.: Princeton University Press, 1967), 224–25. Reprinted by permission of Princeton University Press.

2. Points adapted from Malcom S. Knowles, *Informal Adult Education* (New York: Association Press, 1950), 30–31.

3. Martha Leypoldt, *40 Ways to Teach in Groups* (Valley Forge, Pa.: Judson Press, 1992), 19.

Chapter 25

Methods for Effective Storytelling

"Once upon a time..."

That is one of the most tantalizing phrases in our language. Whose ears don't perk up when they hear that? At the sound of those words we know we're in for something exciting and our imaginations are taken captive. One of the most powerful teaching methods the teacher can use is storytelling. Jesus knew this, and storytelling seems to have been one of his favorite teaching methods.

Stories are essential for describing the Christian experience. Stories were used by Jesus to describe masterfully what our relationship to God could be. Customarily, Jesus used vivid imagery drawn from the everyday life of his listeners. Until the time of the printed text, and the Reformation shortly after, symbols, images (e.g., stained-glass windows, icons, sculpted relief, and art), and storytelling were the main means of communicating the Gospels.

One of the powers in story is the use of symbol. Carl Jung argued that the content of a symbol cannot be fully grasped or expressed in rational terms.[1] He called symbols the transcendent function that helps in the process of individuation — the union of opposites and the healing of the divided self. In terms of Christian teaching for faith development, methods like storytelling, which help learners make connections between symbols and the experiences in their lives, are the most effective for spiritual development.

Yet this simple but powerful method scares more new teachers than any other teaching method. Fortunately, effective storytelling is a skill that anyone can develop.

Choose the Right Story

One day, while discussing favorite stories and movies with my two boys, I offhandedly mentioned that I had read somewhere that there are only eight basic story types (or plots) in the world. Supposedly, all stories derive from these eight basic types. They challenged me to name the eight. I couldn't remember them all, but together we came up with these five basic types of stories (you'll have to see if you can find the other three; we couldn't):

The "plot" story: Plot refers to the plan of action of a story. These stories can be complex and may contain subplots. The story conveys a strong sense of direction in which all of the story elements are leading to a climax. The story of Joseph is an example of a classic plot story.

The problem story: This type of story centers around a problem that needs to be solved. The problem can seem unsolvable, it may center around a dilemma, and often it is resolved through the use of paradox. The story of the Good Samaritan and of King Solomon and the disputed baby are good examples of this type of story.

The quest story: Quest stories are favorites with children and young people. They involve the search for something. Normally, the characters in the story know what they are looking for. The biblical story of the Magi, and classic stories about the search for the Holy Grail are good examples.

The journey story: Like the quest story, this is a travel story, but in this case, characters often do not know what they are searching for. Their ultimate destination, and what they will find when they get there, is uncertain until the conclusion of the narrative. Some examples of the journey story are the wilderness wandering of the people of Israel, the flight to Egypt of Joseph and Mary, and Abraham's early years when he left his home in Ur of the Chaldeans.

The character story: This story centers around a central figure who can be a protagonist or antagonist — or both. The story usually centers on an event that changes the character in the end. The story of Zaccheus is a delightful character story.

Prepare and Practice Your Story

True story: I once got off the subway in New York City on my way to a concert. Not knowing exactly where I was, I approached one of New York's finest and asked, "How do I get to Carnegie Hall?"

He stared at me for a moment and then replied, "Practice, practice, practice." Old joke, but I set myself up for it. Unless you're a natural, becoming a good storyteller requires practice.

Identify where the story is going. In the teaching context, a story is told with a purpose: it supports what you want your learners to learn. What purpose will your story serve in the teaching process?

Outline the story. A strong outline will help you stay on track with the story's development. The sequence of the story is critical, so making an outline will help your learners follow the story. Many classic stories start with the familiar and move to the fantastic. In C. S. Lewis's classic fairy tale for adults, he starts his unsuspecting readers among quiet and familiar surroundings and then plunges them into new worlds in outer space.[2]

Practice telling the story. If possible, practice in front of a mirror or use a tape recorder. Often, what we think we sound like isn't how we actually come across. Practice using a variety of voice tones. Practice sounding enthusiastic. Match the pace of the movement of the story using voice inflection and speed. Use repetition for emphasis and pauses for dramatic effect. The more you practice, the more natural you'll sound when telling the story. Poor storytelling is more of a distraction than a teaching help.

Capture interest at the start. Beginning a good story well is critical, and there are endless ways of doing it. You can begin with a bang (literally) or a whisper. You can use the classic, "Once upon a time..." or ask a question like "Did this ever happen to you?" Once, with a challenging group of children, I started a story by saying, "I'm going to tell you an interesting story, and at the end I'm going to ask one question. I want to see who can answer it!" They were spellbound and attentive, and in the end, they were able to answer the question.

Focus Your Story

Keep your story brief. A good rule of thumb is to limit your story to one minute for each year of your listener's age. Just like in good teaching, your story should be about one thing — and one thing only. Unless there is a reason to do so in support of your lesson, avoid including a story within a story. Stick to the point and keep it short.

Involve Your Learners in Discovery

Storytelling is an interactive method. Engage your learners as participants in the story. When you help your learners move from being passive listeners to active participants in the story, you give them the skill that will allow them to make connections to the biblical stories. You can involve your learners in the story by practicing the following:

- *Make learners feel comfortable.* Give attention to physical comfort as well as providing an emotionally inviting atmosphere.

- *Be natural.* Tell the story your own way, in your own voice, and in your own style. Trying to be like someone else will only serve to distract from the story.

- *Maintain eye contact.* Bring your learners into the story and keep their attention by directing the story at them.

- *Be creative with interruptions.* Incorporate interruptions and fidgety listeners into the story.

- *Use your voice.* Vary your inflection, tone, volume, and pace to match the story action. If the story calls for

---

Planning Your Story Sequence

- *Introduction:* Get their attention!

- *Setting:* Where?

- *Character:* Who?

- *Action:* Where are we going with this?

- *Conflict:* What's the problem?

- *Climax:* Crisis and resolution.

- *Conclusion:* Bring it home; what does it mean?

- *Listener response:* Get feedback and involve the learner.

---

singing, then sing! Use tone changes for different characters to match their personalities.

- *Use dialogue.* Dialogue can make your stories come alive and give your characters personality.

- *Use props.* Simple props can be important focal points for your story. They can help your learners follow the story. Remember that in storytelling, your body is a prop. Use it!

Learning to tell a story — simple or complex — will give you one of the most powerful teaching methods any teacher can have. But as with any skill, practice is the key to success!

Notes

1. Wallace B. Clift, *Jung and Christianity: The Challenge of Reconciliation* (New York: Crossroad, 1982), 81.

2. C. S. Lewis, *Perelandra* (New York: Macmillan, 1965).

Chapter 26

Methods for Critical Thinking

Here's the good news: According to educators Tom and Joani Schultz, 35 percent of fifth- and sixth-graders say their church classes make them think.[1]

Here's the bad news: That may mean that 65 percent of the classes for this age group do not make them think!

Helping learners develop critical thinking in relation to their faith is a significant component of an effective Christian teaching. Critical thinking is characterized by the desire to go beyond uncritical statements and questions that only answer who, when, and where. The critical thinker wants to know the why, how, what for, and so what of things. Critical thinking is the ability to reflect on the operational assumptions that underlie our actions and beliefs. It enables us to be open to new ways of seeing our world and frees us to respond to it in new and different ways.

Imagine for a moment standing in front of a classroom of learners who continually ask you why, how, what for, and so what. Feeling a little uncomfortable imagining what that might be like? If so, then you can see the reason most teachers don't want critical thinkers in their classes — they're troublemakers! Fearing the challenge of having to deal with critical thinkers, most of us are content with having a group of passive learners — those who will accept what we say without question, who will take our word for it, who won't challenge facts, question concepts, seek motives, or dig deeper than what surface knowledge offers.

Passive and uncritical learners may make for model classroom pupils, but they don't make for mature Christians. Can you imagine the kind of person that years of uncritical learning experiences will produce? Peter said that Christians should "always be prepared to give an answer to everyone who asks you to give the reason for the hope that you have. But do this with gentleness and respect" (1 Peter 3:15, NIV). An uncritical learner will never be able to do that. More likely than not, these will be persons who lack discernment, who are easily swayed by arguments even contradictory to what they believe, and whose faith is characterized by a dependence on others.

The apostle Paul wrote, "When we were children, we thought and reasoned as children do. But when we grew up, we quit our childish ways" (1 Cor. 13:11, CEV). He warned believers, "My friends, stop thinking like children. Think like mature people" (1 Cor. 14:20, CEV). Teaching for critical thinking creates learners who are more interested in pursuing truth than in defending beliefs. Doubt leads to faith because beliefs are good only for their time. Think about it, do you believe everything the same way as you did ten years ago? Twenty? Did you not have to let go of uncritical beliefs in order to move on in your faith pilgrimage? The tragic truth is that over a third of adults in our congregations still operate out of an adolescent faith; remaining uncritical, they have never grown beyond the level of thinking and belief they possessed in high school. For them, faith becomes a stagnant habit of the mind rather than a dynamic, ever growing effectual force in their lives.

For the mature learner, being shown you're wrong is a delight. Part of growth is to perpetually realize that now you're in possession of new truth, insight, and understanding, when previously you were mistaken in what you believed. Seeking truth becomes a part of your identity. A healthy faith does not make beliefs such a part of self that one's identity in vested in them. A mature faith is iconoclastic; it seeks innovative ways of thinking about established ideas. Critical thinkers dislike being in a spiritual rut and welcome new ways of seeing things and understanding faith. They are continually looking for new facts and perspectives to test current thought and challenge belief.

Dialogue

Critical thinking is best learned in the process of dialogue. Engaging in open dialogue enables the learner to:

- accept responsibility for his or her own thoughts
- challenge new ideas
- discern the worth and validity of current beliefs
- rethink established ideas and beliefs
- ask deeper questions for higher order learning
- reflect on the thinking process

Below are some techniques to help your learners engage in critical thinking during your teaching-learning experiences:

- Ask lots of open-ended questions that don't have a right/ wrong, or yes/no answer: "What if...", "What would you do...?" "Why do you think...?"

- Allow time for learner responses. Ask your question, and then shut your mouth and wait for the learner response. Silence does not mean that nothing is happening; it means that learners are thinking. When a learner responds to your question, allow at least five seconds before responding. This gives other learners a chance to think about the question and their response in the dialogue process.

- Continue the dialogue with follow-up questions. Some examples are "Let me hear more"; "How did you arrive at that conclusion?" "How did you know that?" "Did you just think about that or is that something you knew?"

- Avoid evaluating learners' discussion responses that are wrong or off the mark (but never ignore a response). Respond with "okay," "thank you," or "uh-huh." Or try my favorite honest response, "Hmm. That's interesting. I've never thought of it that way before." Deflect the response to include other learners by asking, "Does everybody agree with that?" or "Does everybody think that's completely accurate?" or "Interesting answer. Can anyone think of how someone might challenge that thought?" Doing this allows learners time to think and respond, as well as giving permission to share thoughts and ideas still in progress. There are no "wrong answers" in dialogue — a wrong answer is part of the process necessary to get to better answers or better questions.

- Encourage guesses. Guesses are cognitive movements toward sharper conclusions. However, help your learners know the difference between a wild, uncritical guess and an informed guess. Ask, "Is that a hunch?" "Does anybody feel one way or the other about that?"

- Encourage learner questions. A critical thinker's greatest ability is knowing how to ask right or better questions. Dialogue will encourage your learners to ask questions of you as teacher and of the other learners.

- Challenge your learners to embrace dissonance — that uncomfortable feeling one gets when new ideas are entertained that challenge familiar ways of thinking and living. Encourage them to recognize it for what it is, a first step to growth and learning as the old and familiar are forced to accommodate the new and unknown.

Teaching for critical thinking will challenge the teacher to focus more on the learning process and less on information sharing. Information in and of itself is meaningless. Facts don't change lives. Helping learners know how to think critically about information, beliefs, and behaviors helps them be more discerning Christians. Critical thinking helps learners understand that in matters of faith it's not what you believe, it's how. Many people believe that Jesus is the Son of God (the Bible says that even the demons believe that). But what difference does accepting that information as fact make in the life of a person? For those who merely give assent to it: none. For those

---

Methods for Critical Thinking

- Outlining
- Graphing and extrapolating
- Summarizing
- Interpreting
- Relating
- Classifying
- Researching

- Evaluating
- Identifying fact or opinion
- Generalizing
- Drawing parallels
- Self-correcting
- Applying criteria
- Hypothesizing

---

who have critically wrestled with what that means for them: everything! That is the difference that a critical faith makes!

Note

1. Tom and Joani Schultz, *Why Nobody Learns Much of Anything at Church and How to Fix It* (Loveland, Colo.: Group Publisher, 1993), 88.

Chapter 27

Methods for Jump-Starting Creativity

It happens to all of us: there's a lesson to be taught, a speech to make, a project to begin, or an article to write — and the deadline is rushing at us like an out of control tractor-trailer that's jumped the median onto our lane and is heading straight for us. Despite the looming prospect of disaster, we seem unable to come up with an idea for a story, a theme, or a teaching technique to bring home the point. We're stuck and blocked!

You know what I mean if you're a Sunday school teacher. Sunday morning comes around every week. For every lesson we're expected to deliver the goods. Our learners expect us to entertain as well as to teach, to be insightful, present a "new" truth in creative ways, and maintain a level of enthusiasm usually allowed only to the most manic of stand-up comics.

At times we need techniques to jump-start our creativity — something to get the cerebral neurons firing at a higher rate than the atomic particles in molasses on a cold winter day.

Here are two techniques I use to get the creative juices flowing when my mind can't break through the sludge of cerebral myelin and sluggish, oxygen-deprived Schwann cells (look it up if you'd like).

Alphabet Brainstorming

Alphabet brainstorming is a variation of the familiar brainstorming technique you use with your learners when guiding them to explore ideas and options. But in this technique, rather than starting with a blank piece of paper or flip chart, you write the letters of the alphabet down the left side of the sheet from top to bottom. You don't have to write the whole alphabet, but the more letters you get on the paper, the better.

Next, write your topic or project on the top as a header, and starting with the letter A at the top of the sheet, jot down as many words and phrases that come to mind that start with that letter. Separate each with a comma on the same line until you run out of room, then move on to the next line and do the same with the letter B.

Continue this way until you fill the page or run out of letters. Chances are you'll come up with a couple of ideas to get you going on your project. While fighting a deadline for a newsletter article, I found myself "stuck" with no idea of what I was going to write about. The more I thought about it, the more frustrated I became. I sat staring at the computer monitor so long I eventually was able to confirm that my monitor had 1024 pixels on the horizontal and 768 vertical lines.

I decided to use the alphabet brainstorming method. First, I wrote down a title for the exercise, "Newsletter Article." Next, I quickly jotted down whatever came to mind next to the letters on the left side of the paper and came up with the list shown in the box below. Next, I examined the words on the sheet and

---

Alphabet Brainstorming

NEWSLETTER ARTICLE

A	alligators, alliteration, always, achievement, activity
B	becoming, brainstorming, best, believers
C	cannibals, caution, creativity, cartoons, croutons
D	deliver, decisions, design, driving, don'ts
E	entertainment, ecstasy, environment
F	feelings, forever, fever, favorites, faith
G	government, grateful, going, goobers, great
H	habits, health, heaven, having, heat, hover

looked for those that somehow connected in my mind. I circled "activity," "brainstorming," "creativity," and "decisions." After just a few moments of pondering on how those words connected I had my idea for the newsletter. Soon, I had a finished article on using the method of alphabet brainstorming for jump-starting creativity.

Play "What If..."

Another powerful way to get unstuck is to play "What if...." This creativity starter works by forcing you to break through assumptions and self-imposed limitations. It lets you see things differently from your customary ways.

Think about or look at the problem you're trying to solve. Then ask yourself "What if..." questions about all aspects of the problem: yourself, your learners, your room, your environment, your teaching methods, your lesson plan, the sound of your voice, your dress, the hour or the day...everything!

For example:

- What if you taught the class entirely in made-up sign language?

- What if you taught your adult class this week's lesson using the children's teaching procedures?

- What if you rearranged the chairs in the class so that your learners all sat in a circle...facing outward?

- What if you pretended you were a biblical scholar when teaching the Bible passage — and believed it?

- What if this were the last lesson you will ever teach?

- What if you knew that what you will teach next Sunday will change the life of one of your students forever?

- What if getting into heaven depended on how well you taught your students?

- What if you lived in the poorest country in the world and had no teaching materials? How would you optimize learning for your students?

- What if all Bibles disappeared today? How well would you be prepared to teach on Sunday?

- What if everyone on your class roll showed up on Sunday?

- What if you prepared for your class on Sunday afternoon instead of Saturday? (Sorry, I just had to get that one in.)

Two final words on creativity blockers. One of the most notorious creativity blockers is when we convince ourselves that "I am not a creative person." Everyone is creative to some degree — and can be more creative. Sometimes the first step is just telling yourself that you are indeed a creative person.[1]

Second, according to Robert Friedel, who has studied creativity in history's most celebrated inventors, creativity almost always hinges on creative observation. He argues that the history of invention may have progressed as much by creative accidents as by rigorous scientific genius.[2] Being creative may just be a matter of being able to see things a little differently.

When the deadlines loom close and creativity seems to be a lost skill, shake yourself up by using alphabet brainstorming or "What if...." Don't hesitate to use these methods in your teaching. I've used them to help get committees unstuck and to force learners to think "outside the lines."

Notes

1. Roger Von Oach, *A Whack on the Side of the Head: How You Can Be More Creative* (New York: Warner Books, 1983).

2. Robert Friedel, "The Accidental Inventor," *Discover* (October 1996): 58–69.

Chapter 28

Methods for Process Learning

I've found the perfect solution for every church's nominating committee teacher-recruitment dilemma. Whenever a committee member corners an unsuspecting member who pleads, "But I don't know how to teach," he or she will reply with this sure-fire recruitment answer: "Good! You're just the kind of teacher we want!"

What terrifies most would-be teachers, and even some experienced teachers, is the idea of having to perform well in the classroom. This is a symptom of the belief that in the teaching-learning process the teacher's ability to "teach" is most important. The truth, however, is that it is the learner's participation in the learning experience that is the key to effective learning. When the emphasis is on teacher performance rather than learning, we may wind up creating passive and dependent learners. One of the most successful ways of becoming an effective teacher is to change your focus from teaching to learning.

Below are three methods for process teaching that place the focus on the learning experience as opposed to teaching performance: the MUD, the LEGO, and the GAPS. All of these methods are process-oriented and call for the learners to take primary responsibility for their own learning. The role of the teacher in this teaching approach is that of facilitator. During process learning, the specific teacher functions include:

- monitoring the learning process

- maintaining a learning environment

- providing the resources for learning

- monitoring group time

- guiding toward a learning conclusion

The MUD Method

"MUD" stands for Memorizing, Understanding, and Doing.[1] In this approach learners take responsibility for their learning by deciding for themselves to memorize facts, understand concepts, and do a physical learning activity. The role of the teacher is to facilitate and encourage the application of these three components by organizing the content of the lesson. This learning-focused approach looks like this:

1. *Brief content lecture.* The lecture is no more than five to seven minutes in length and serves only to provide the context and direction of the learning experience.

2. *Small group process stage.* The class is divided into small groups. The groups examine content material from which the learners will generate concepts. The teacher provides content material (a Bible passage, a story, an article), and challenges the groups to identify key concepts presented in the material. They choose a portion of the content to commit to memory (a verse, a phrase, or a quote).

3. *Small group planning stage.* The groups work on reaching a consensus on how they want to achieve an understanding of the concept. The teacher provides a worksheet to keep the groups focused (worksheets should contain open-ended questions for exploration and discussion in addition to any ground rules the groups need to observe).

4. *Exploration and pondering stage.* The groups work at exploring, clarifying, defining, and understanding the concept. The handout suggests ways of doing this: defining, research, comparing and contrasting, illustrating, etc.

5. *Discussion, summary, and handouts.* The teacher gathers the small groups together as a class. Group members share the portion memorized and the rationale for their choice. The teacher leads them in a discussion of the concepts explored and summarizes the learning experience. A final summary handout is given to the class.

The LEGO Method

"LEGO" stands for Lecture, Experience Groups, Outcome. In this method small groups share life experiences in order to arrive at the desired outcome. In this way, the content of the lesson becomes the lives of the learners themselves. The teacher helps make connections between content (the lives of the learners) and the topic under consideration (the focus or theme).

Here is a sample of the LEGO method I used recently in dealing with the topic of transitions. Learners were given a handout with the four discussion questions plus background content information. The learning process looked like this:

1. The teacher presents a brief lecture (ten minutes) on transitions in the development of the computer to help define and illustrate the theme (see the box below).

Development of the Computer Outline

1830s Charles Babbage builds the first "real" computer. Lack of ability to mass produce it coupled with a lack of understanding of the nature of electricity hinder any further progress.

1850s George Boole invents binary math.

1947 Transistors are invented and replace vacuum tubes. Integrated circuit developed.

1975 Microcomputer invented.

Examples of societal impact of the development of the computer.

---

2. The class is divided into pairs, which are given a few minutes to discuss the first question:

   - *"Name two of the most significant events in world history, and for each identify one way in which the world was changed because of it."*

Time is called and responses are listed on the board. Questions are asked by the teacher:

   - How many are in the twentieth century?
   - How many had global impact?
   - Any others not listed?
   - Which are the three most significant? Why?

3. The class is divided into groups of three for the remainder of the process. They are given a few minutes to discuss the next question:

   - *"What has been the most significant societal development that has had an impact on your life in the past ten years? twenty years? thirty years?"*

Time is called and a short debriefing follows.

4. The teacher shares some content to provide a reference for the next step. The content is a brief list on transition that is on their handout (see the box below).

The Nature of Transitions

1. May be instigated by nodal (instigating) events.
2. May be a result of natural development or of crises.
3. Require time.
4. Require giving up something.
5. Require redefining "normal."
6. Require creativity and imagination.

5. The groups are instructed to answer the following questions, which bring the matter of transition to a more personal level:

- *"Name one significant transition in your family of origin. With your group members, share the following: (1) Who was affected most by the transition? (2) How did it feel in the midst of the transition? (3) How did your family deal creatively with the transition? (4) At the end of the transition, what was 'new' for your family?"*

Time is called and groups are asked to answer the final question on their handout:

- *"Think about your church or another faith community you have been a part of. Identify a significant event that caused a transition stage. With your group, discuss the following: (1) Was the transition a result of crisis? (2) Who provided leadership during the transition? (3) Contrast the feelings and thoughts at the beginning of the transition with those at the conclusion of the transition. (4) When did the church know that the transition period ended? (5) What is the most important lesson you can share about how the church handled that transition?"*

6. During the Outcome stage, each group is asked to share their responses to the last question. These "most important lessons" are listed on a flip chart and discussed.

Notice that in these methods, there is minimal "teaching" but a maximizing of participatory learning. The teacher functions as a facilitator for the learning experience by structuring the learning process and making content available for exploration, not explanation.

The GAPS Method

The GAPS (Group Activity Problem Solving) approach is ideal for a group of learners who can take on a high degree of responsibility for their learning. This problem-based learning method will strengthen the self-directed learning skills of the learners.

The role of the teacher is to provide a simulated problem in the area of study for the group and provide some of the resources the group may need to solve the problem. First, the teacher presents the problem to the learners, and they work as a group to set up the learning objectives and expectations for the group. This important first step helps the learners determine what they need to learn and leads them to identify the kinds of information they will have to gather. Through consensus, the group fine-tunes their understanding of the problem and clarifies the information they need to reach a solution. The group members do research and critique their sources of information, which they bring back to the group. When the group reconvenes they work together on a solution and assess their learning.

In the final step of this learning process, the teacher debriefs the learners by leading them to summarize what they have learned and to reflect on how they went about solving the problem.

The learning process may look like this:

1. The teacher presents a problem to be solved based on the study content.

2. The group determines their learning objectives (what they want to have learned at the end of the experience).

3. The group decides on their expectations about the learning experience.

4. The group works to reach consensus on the nature of the problem and the kind of information they need to solve the problem.

5. Members of the group identify which resources they will use to find the information needed.

6. Members do research and critique the sources of information.

7. The group reconvenes and attempts to solve the problem with the information they've gathered.

8. The teacher helps the group debrief the learning experience.

Using the MUD, LEGO, and GAPS methods, a good teacher can actually teach more by performing less. In changing the focus from teaching to learning, the learners take greater responsibility for their own learning through increased participation in all stages of the learning process.

Becoming a very good teacher is one of those lifelong projects that engage us on journeys of self-discovery and self-mastery. Unlike other crafts that also require competence, teaching calls for much more. Our craft of Christian teaching is not merely performance, because it flows out of being — who we are and what we believe. More than technical skills are needed to be an effective Christian teacher: we are called to be competent but passionate, knowledgeable but humble. Ultimately, it's not what we know that makes us very good teachers; rather, it's who we know — the Master Teacher himself. To the extent that we know him is the extent to which we become very good Christian teachers.

Note

1. See Cheryl Harrison, "Learning Management," *ERIC Digest*, no. 73 (1988), ERIC Clearinghouse on Adult, Career, and Vocational Education, ERIC Document Reproduction Service No. ED296121. This is a modified version of the MUD approach developed by Sylvia Downs in "Developing Learning Skills." The GAPS method is based on the work of Howard S. Barrows in "Learning Management in the Context of Small Group Problem-based Learning" as presented in Harrison's article.

Appendixes

Cognitive Learning Actions

Learning Level	Learning Actions		
KNOWLEDGE	know	define	memorize
	repeat	record	list
	recall	name	relate
	collect	label	specify
	cite	tell	enumerate
	recount		
COMPREHENSION	restate	summarize	discuss
	describe	recognize	explain
	express	identify	locate
	report	retell	review
	translate		
APPLICATION	exhibit	solve	interview
	simulate	apply	employ
	use	dramatize	demonstrate
	practice	operate	illustrate
	experiment	calculate	show
ANALYSIS	interpret	analyze	diagram
	compare	contrast	categorize
	scrutinize	probe	investigate
	discover	inquire	detect
	inspect	classify	arrange
	group	organize	examine
	survey	dissect	inventory
	differentiate		
SYNTHESIS	compose	plan	propose
	produce	invent	develop
	design	formulate	arrange
	assemble	construct	create
	prepare	imagine	hypothesize
	predict	originate	generalize
	contrive	concoct	systematize
	incorporate		
EVALUATION	judge	decide	appraise
	evaluate	rate	compare
	value	revise	conclude
	select	criticize	assess
	measure	estimate	infer
	deduce	score	predict
	choose	recommend	determine

Learner Participation Methods

Use the following checklists to find those methods that will help your students become participants in the learning process. Every time you use one of the methods listed below, check off a box. As you check off the methods you use, you'll discover those you most depend on and you will be able to challenge yourself to experiment with other methods.

VERBAL METHODS

Brainstorming															
Buzz groups															
Case studies															
Circle response															
Conversation															
Debate															
Discussion															
Forum															
Free association															
Interview															
Interview-report															
Lecture															
Listening teams															
Memorization															
Open-ended case study															
Panel															
Personal experience (share)															
Problem solving															
Problem-issue research															
Pro-con analysis															
Question and answer															
Reaction panel															
Research report															
Resource persons															
Retelling and resequencing															
Storytelling															
Study teams															
Testimony															
Testing															
Word association															
Written response(s)															

ART METHODS

Block painting													
Blow painting													
Bulletin board													
Cartoon/comic strips													
Clay sculpting													
Coat of arms													
Collage													
Crayon etchings													
Crayon resist													
Crayon rubbings													
Diorama													
Dough sculpture													
Drawing													
Exhibit													
Finger painting													
Frieze													
Gadget painting													
Illustration													
Map													
Melted crayons													
Mobile													
Montage													
Mosaic													
Mural													
Paper tearing/cutting													
Papier-mâché													
Picture study													
Poster													
Puppet making													
Rebus													
Sand painting													
Spatter painting													
Sponge painting													
Stitchery													
String painting													
Tempera painting													
Thematic apperception													
TV box													

DRAMA METHODS

Acting out a Bible event														
Choral speaking														
Contemporary Bible skit														
Dialogue														
Discussion starter														
Dramatic interviews														
Monologue														
Pantomime														
Puppets														
Radio and TV format														
Role playing														

MUSIC METHODS

Group singing														
Hymn reading														
Hymn-text study														
Lyric writing														
Recordings														

PAPER AND PENCIL METHODS

Charts															
Creative writing															
dialogue															
diary															
drawing															
journal															
letters															
monologue															
newspaper articles															
paraphrase															
poetry: free verse															
poetry: topic poem															
Graph															
Jot sheet															
Map															
Notebook															
Puzzle															
acrostic															
coded message															
crossword															
Quizzes															
definitions															
fill in the blanks															
matching items															
multiple choice															
open-ended statements															
pretest															
posttest															
true-false statements															
Sentence response															
Time line															
Unsigned written responses															
Worksheet, handouts															

VISUALS

Nonprojected visual																
learning center																
objects, models																
poster																
Projected visual																
computer generated																
films																
overhead projector																
shadow puppet show																
slides																
video conferencing																
videos																

PERSONAL EXPERIENCE METHODS

Outreach visitation																
Personal witnessing																
Ministry project																
Fellowship gathering																
Mentoring																
Games																
Bible baseball																
Bible football																
Bible Jeopardy																
Bible Linko																
Bible word games																
Board games																
Clothespin Bible verse																
Concentration																
Scrambled verse																
Secret codes																
Simulation games																
Sorting games																
Spin and go																
String-a-match																
Surprise picture																
Throw-catch-answer																
Tic-tac-toe																

Appendix C

A Model for Church Life as Curriculum

ONGOING BODY LIFE (congregational) ACTIONS:

The congregational themes flow out of the binding core of the faith community, the church covenant or mission statement. They help give focus to particular covenant emphases throughout the church year. Every theme should contain *each* of the following church actions (functions) expressed in manners that highlight the congregational theme for that period. Ideally, all programming and activities will flow naturally and holistically from the themes, leading to a balanced approach to activities, programs, sermon themes, worship services, educational opportunities, etc.

- ADORATION (worship)
- TELLING (proclamation and witness)
- EDUCATION (instruction, discipleship, and nurture)
- COMMUNION (fellowship)
- OUTREACH (inclusiveness and invitation)
- SERVING (mission and missions)
- NETWORKING (associations and extended community)

**Special thanks to Vienna Baptist Church, Vienna, Va., and First Baptist Church of Chattanooga, Chattanooga, Tenn.

Months	Congregational Themes	Church Year	Programs & Events
September–October	"Growth in Faith"	*Pentecost to Kingdomtide*	• Promotion Sunday • Youth Kick-off • Sunday School Picnic • Business Meetings • Youth Sunday • Missions Emphasis • Stewardship Emphasis • Diaconate Retreat
November	"Answering Our Call"	*Pentecost*	• Pledge Sunday • World Hunger Emphasis • Creativity Retreat • Women's Retreat • Fall Drama • Youth Retreat
Thanksgiving–January 3	"Holy Days & Holidays"	*Thanksgiving, Advent, Christmas, New Year*	• Thanksgiving Program • Christmas Workshop • Christmas Programs • Twelfth Night
January–February	"Word & Witness"	*Epiphany*	• Family Retreat • Missions Emphasis • Budget Adopted • Youth Choir Retreat • Youth Drama-Musical
March–April	"Spirituality & Victory"	*Lent, Easter*	• Diaconate Retreat • Gifts Sunday • Discipleship Classes • Teacher Training • Lenten Studies • Seder Supper • Tenebrae Service • Palm Sunday • Good Friday • Easter • Baptisms • Memorial Sunday • Children's Sunday • Men's Retreat
May–June	"Family & Faith"	*Pentecost*	• Women's Retreat • Mother's Day • Family Dedications • Dramas/Musicals • Art Show • Leadership Appreciation Banquet • Parenting Workshop • Father's Day • Marriage Enrichment Retreat • Business Meeting • Choir Recognition Program
July–August	"Sabbath & Service"	*Pentecost*	• Vacation Bible School • Children's Camp • Summer Camp Program • Theater workshop • Leadership Retreat • Teacher Orientation

Bibliography

Archambault, R. D. "The Concept of Need and Its Relation to Certain Aspects of Educational Theory," *Harvard Educational Review* (1957): 27.

Ausubel, David P. *The Psychology of Meaningful Verbal Learning.* New York: Grune & Stratton, 1963.

————. "The Use of Advanced Organizers in the Learning and Retention of Meaningful Verbal Material," *Journal of Educational Psychology* 51 (1966): 267–72.

Baker, Augusta, and Ellin Greene. *Storytelling: Art and Technique.* New York: R. R. Bowker Company, 1987.

Benson, Peter L., and Carolyn H. Eklin. *Effective Christian Education: A National Study of Protestant Congregations: A Summary Report on Faith, Loyalty, and Congregational Life.* Search Institute, March 1990.

Bloom, Benjamin, and Associates. *Taxonomy of Educational Objectives: Handbook 1: Cognitive Domain.* New York: David McKay Co., 1956.

Bruce, Debra Fulghum. "Key to Learning: Small Groups," *Church Educator* 19, no. 7 (July 1994): 27–30.

Bruner, Jerome S. "The Act of Discovery," *Harvard Educational Review* (1961): 21–23.

————. *The Process of Education.* Cambridge: Harvard University Press, 1961.

————. *Toward a Theory of Instruction.* Cambridge: Harvard University Press, 1966.

Clark, C. M., and R. J. Yinger. *Three Studies of Teacher Planning.* Institute for Research on Teaching, Research Series No. 55. East Lansing: Michigan State University, 1979.

Clift, Wallace B. *Jung and Christianity: The Challenge of Reconciliation.* New York: Crossroad, 1982.

DeCecco, John P., and William R. Crawford. *The Psychology of Learning and Instruction: Educational Psychology.* 2d ed. Englewood Cliffs, N.J.: Prentice-Hall, 1968.

Dillon, J. T. *Questioning and Teaching: A Manual of Practice.* New York: Teachers College Press, 1988.

Eisner, E. W. "Educational Objectives: Help or Hindrance?" *School Review* (Autumn 1967): 250–66.

Ennis, Robert H. "A Taxonomy of Critical Thinking Dispositions and Abilities," in *Teaching Thinking Skills: Theory and Practice*. Ed. Joan Boykoff Baron and Robert J. Sternberg. New York: Freeman, 1987.

Foust, Dennis W. "Curriculum Engineering in the Local Church: A Contextual Model." Ed.D. dissertation, Southern Baptist Theological Seminary, 1988.

Fowler, James. *Becoming Adult, Becoming Christian: Adult Development and Christian Faith*. New York: Harper & Row, 1986.

Friedel, Robert. "The Accidental Inventor," *Discovery* (October 1996): 58–69.

Gagné, Robert. *The Conditions of Learning and Theory of Instruction*. New York: Rinehart and Winston, 1970.

Gangel, Kenneth, and Howard Hendricks. *The Christian Educator's Handbook on Teaching*. Wheaton, Ill.: Victor Books, a division of Scripture Press Publications, 1988.

Gardner, Howard. *Frames of Mind, Multiple Intelligences: The Theory in Practice*. New York: Basic Books, 1983.

———. *The Unschooled Mind: How Children Think and How Schools Should Teach*. New York: Basic Books, 1991.

Glenn, H. Stephen, and Jane Nelson. *Raising Children for Success*. Fair Oaks, Calif.: Sunrise Press, 1987.

Gregory, John Milton. *The Seven Laws of Teaching*. Grand Rapids: Baker Book House, 1979.

Harrison, Cheryl. "Learning Management," *ERIC Digest*, no. 73 (1988), ERIC Clearinghouse on Adult, Career, and Vocational Education. ERIC Document Reproduction Service No. ED296161.

Kelsey, Morton. *Can Christians Be Educated? A Proposal for Effective Communication of Our Christian Religion*. Comp. and ed. Harold William Burgess. Birmingham: Religious Education Press, 1977.

Knowles, Malcom S. *Informal Adult Education*. New York: Association Press, 1950.

Lefrançois, Guy R. *Psychology for Teaching*. Belmont, Calif.: Wadsworth Publishing Company, 1979.

Leypoldt, Martha M. *40 Ways to Teach in Groups*. Valley Forge, Pa.: Judson Press, 1967.

Master Notes: Stewardship Resources for Church Leaders 6, no. 2 (1995).

McCutcheon, G. "How Do Elementary School Teachers Plan Their Courses?" *Elementary School Journal* 81 (1980): 4–23.

McKenzie, Leon. "Developmental Spirituality and the Religious Educator," in *The Spirituality of the Religious Educator*. Ed. James Michael Lee. Birmingham: Religious Education Press, 1985.

McNabb, Bill, and Steven Mabry. *Teaching the Bible Creatively*. Grand Rapids: Zondervan, 1990.

Muirhead, Ian A. *Education in the New Testament.* New York: Association Press, 1965.

Osmer, Richard Robert. *Teaching for Faith: A Guide for Teachers of Adult Classes.* Louisville: Westminster/John Knox Press, 1992.

Peterson, P. L., et al. "Teacher Planning, Teacher Behavior, and Student Achievement," *American Educational Research Journal* (1978).

Raths, L., M. Harmin, and S. Simon. *Values and Teaching: Working with Values in the Classroom.* Columbus, Ohio: Charles E. Merrill, 1966.

Richards, Lawrence O. *Creative Bible Teaching.* Chicago: Moody Press, 1970.

Seymour, Jack L., and Donald E. Miller. *Contemporary Approaches to Christian Education.* Nashville: Abingdon Press, 1982.

Schultz, Tom and Joani. *Why Nobody Learns Much of Anything at Church and How to Fix It.* Loveland, Colo.: Group Publisher, 1993.

Treston, Kevin. *A New Vision of Religious Education.* Mystic, Conn.: Twenty-Third Publications, 1993.

Von Oach, Roger. *A Whack on the Side of the Head: How You Can Be More Creative.* New York: Warner Books, 1983.

Wilhelm, Richard. *The I-Ching, or Book of Changes.* Trans. Cary F. Baynes, Bollingen Series 19, 3d ed. Princeton: Princeton University Press, 1967.

Index